The Motivation of Politicians

The Motivation of Politicians

James L. Payne
Oliver H. Woshinsky
Eric P. Veblen
William H. Coogan
Gene E. Bigler

NELSON-HALL PUBLISHERS
Chicago

LIBRARY OF CONGRESS CATALOGING IN PUBLICATION DATA

Main entry under title:

The motivation of politicians.

  Bibliography: p.
  Includes index.
  1. Political psychology. 2. Politicians—Psychology.
I. Payne, James L.
JA74.5.M66 1984   320'.1'9   83-26853
ISBN 0-8304-1038-4 (cloth)
ISBN 0-88229-824-0 (paper)

Copyright ©1984 by James L. Payne

All rights reserved. No part of this book may be reproduced in any form without permission in writing from the publisher, except by a reviewer who wishes to quote brief passages in connection with a review written for broadcast or for inclusion in a magazine or newspaper. For information address Nelson-Hall Inc., Publishers, 111 North Canal Street, Chicago, Illinois 60606.

Manufactured in the United States of America

10 9 8 7 6 5 4 3 2 1

The paper in this book is pH neutral (acid free).

Contents

1 Introduction   1

2 The Status Incentive   19
   I. David Clark: "Like Being Avis"   21
   II. William Jennings Bryan: "The Lure of the College Prize"   30

3 The Program Incentive   49
   I. William Hammersmith: "In Morris County… You Can Buy Cigarettes for $2.76 a Carton"   53
   II. Benjamin Franklin: "The Convenience of Having But One Gutter in Such a Narrow Street"   66

4 The Conviviality Incentive   79
   I. Peter Finley: "Satisfaction to Me Comes from Helping People"   81
   II. Brooks Hays: "Wanting to Give Every Student an A"   92

5 The Obligation Incentive   103
   I. Armand Dupuis: "So Maybe I'm Not a Politician"   105
   II. Frederick L. Hackenburg: "A Straight and Narrow Path"   112

6 The Game Incentive   129
   I. Gordon Hart: "I'm Competitive and Love This Kind of Thing"   134

II. Charles B. Lipsen: "I Wanted to Be at the
      Center of the Action" 146
7 The Mission and Adulation Incentives   163
8 Incentives and Political Behavior   169
   Appendix I. Outline of Incentive Characteristics
                as Seen in Interviews   185
   Appendix II. Conducting and Interpreting Incentive
                Interviews   191
Notes   197
Bibliography   203
Index   209

1 Introduction

WE TAKE POLITICIANS FOR granted. Of course we are skeptical about them. We examine their deeds closely; we criticize them freely. But we take their existence for granted. We assume that if an opening occurs for legislator, for commissioner, or for mayor, someone will come forward to seek the post. A factory may announce that it seeks forty welders by July 1. We do not find it unusual if, by that date, it has obtained the services of only sixteen. In politics this parallel is difficult to find. A state government seeks 132 legislators by November 6. On November 7, it has 132 legislators, having turned away many additional applicants.

Why are political offices always filled? Why does the supply of politicians so regularly exceed the demand? Our first supposition might be that political roles are exceedingly pleasant, affording a degree of ease and comfort unsurpassed by other occupations.

The close examination of the politician's life suggests otherwise. Politics is not a cushy, comfortable occupation. To the contrary, the politician's role is unusually stressful and taxing. This observation is significant, for it deepens the mystery of why the supply of politicians is so copious. Let us examine more closely the different types of deprivation that characterize political life.

At the top of the list, we would place the criticism and hostility that inevitably come to the holders of public office. "You can vote fifteen times exactly the way Mr. X thinks you ought to vote," says an Alexandria, Virginia, councilman, "but if the sixteenth time you vote against him, Mr. X is quite likely to call you and not only complain about your vote, but impugn your integrity, your heredity, your fitness for office and everything else."

"I dread answering the phone," says Mike Jacot,* a councilman in Portland, Maine. "I never realized I'd be in a situation where I don't really like answering the phone anymore; it rings so often and so often it's people who are very emotional." Those of us who have been the target of a crank caller can sympathize. We know how irritating, how unnerving such callers can be. Yet we are pestered for only a day or two. Mike has taken several years of crank calls. And he can't leave the phone off the hook. He has to listen. He's a politician.

Private criticism is unpleasant, but more wounding still are the public accusations that abound in politics. It is one thing to be chastised in a personal conversation. Let the same criticism appear in print or in a public assembly, and it becomes graver, more disturbing. The very nature of the politician's role makes him the target of much public rebuke. And, of course, the accusations and complaints are often highly subjective, uninformed, and unfair. Certainly they seem so to the criticized politician.

The antagonism most politicians experience is often more than mere verbal criticism. Political controversies may become highly emotional. People become bitter, enraged, irrational, violent. The politician may find himself the target of obscene phone calls. His wife and children may be threatened. His automobile tires may be slashed. Hal Mason, another Portland councilman, was almost run down by a car—intentionally, he believes. "When I jog," he says, "I carry a club now. I have the last two or three years."

---

*For all interviewed respondents, we have changed names to protect their privacy.

In many foreign lands, politics is much more noticeably dangerous than in the United States: Italy, Iran, Syria, Chile, the Dominican Republic, Rhodesia, Uganda.... Even from a distance, we can see that the risks of political participation in these places include imprisonment and death. The impulse to avoid politics in such settings would seem immense; yet even here one finds a steady stream of seekers after available political offices.

Politicians, then, are the recipients of a steady, corrosive flow of criticism and hostility that would deeply disturb most people; and it disturbs them, too.

A second drawback of politics is the drain on the politician's time. Political roles are open-ended. There is no finite list of tasks to do which, when finished, leave the individual free to do what he pleases. There is no limited time period that defines the work day, outside of which one's time is one's own. In politics there is always more to do: another hearing one could attend, another administrator one should visit, another report to study, another complaint to follow up. Rather like a doctor during an epidemic, the politician is drawn into a level of activity more strenuous than he would like. As a consequence, he feels pressured, unable to devote adequate time to his family, his occupation, or his hobbies.

Furthermore, many of the demands on a politician's time arise irregularly and uncontrollably: a draft proposal is needed tomorrow morning; an emergency evening session of the legislature is called; a constituent wants a meeting at lunch; the phone rings during breakfast. The undefined, irregular nature of the politician's role occasions much inefficiency, much frittering away of time waiting, driving, flying, getting caught in idle conversations. The irregular schedule also militates against the maintenance of healthy habits. Smoking and drinking are more difficult to control. Sleep is shortchanged.

Naturally the level of stress varies, depending on the politician and his particular job. But, with few exceptions, politicians at every level find the time demands and disruptions of political life unpleasant.

A third type of deprivation politicians often experience is financial. It is a popular belief, of course, that politics is a lucrative field, that many politicians are "in it for the money." Our observation of scores of politicians, both in the United States and abroad, suggests that this view is substantially in error. There are, of course, cases of individuals who have made considerable wealth in connection with politics, but they appear to be very much the exception. Typically, being in politics involves a financial sacrifice.

James Douglas is a florist in a large Virginia city. He is also a member of the local city council, where he has been involved in the highly controversial dismissal of the director of public health. "Two people directly told me that they would no longer do business with me because of it. Last month we had an 8 percent decrease in business. Which is hard to take." For businessmen and others who depend on consumer preferences for their livelihood — doctors, lawyers, insurance brokers, real estate dealers — political involvement can turn customers away.

The activities of politics — campaigning, traveling, moving, entertaining, communicating — create unusual expenses, some of which are never reimbursed. For example, politicians are sitting ducks for charities; they are the first to be approached and cannot comfortably decline to give. They are subject to other unusual expenses that the average citizen would not suspect. One Connecticut state legislator told us: "My constituents are always bringing me their traffic tickets. They think I can fix them with the local police. Actually, I just take their tickets and pay the fines myself. It costs me a few bucks, but it's a favor they remember — and they wouldn't believe me if I told them I couldn't fix tickets in this town!"

Furthermore, in giving his time and energy to politics, the politician is foregoing the income-earning opportunity of using his time in another way. Politicians, after all, are energetic individuals with a capacity to appeal to large numbers of people. Their talents would find significant remuneration in other fields, such as business or entertainment. Hence, when we see congressmen or senators, for example, with a salary many times the national average, we should not automatically suppose that politics is financially profitable for them. Most of these individuals, pursuing a private career with the same effort, would typically make more money—and not face the unusual expenses that politics entails.

Holding public office involves certain stresses and sacrifices; even more remarkable, however, are the stresses and sacrifices involved in obtaining public office. If a letter arrived in the mail appointing one of us to fill a congressional seat, most of us would accept the seat and serve—though not for long. But public offices are not obtained by patiently watching the mail. To reach them normally requires a campaign—a sustained, strenuous competition. In this competition the aforementioned deprivations are especially salient: criticism and hostility, time pressures, financial sacrifices. Yet by entering this competition—lasting many weeks and often many months—one is afforded only a chance of winning public office. The campaign typically necessary to obtain public office represents an enormous hurdle: distasteful, often grueling, uncertain of success. People anxious to keep their lives pleasant and comfortable would never undertake it. Yet politicians do.

The paradox is challenging: we never lack politicians, yet being in politics involves substantial personal costs. Clearly, individuals are not attracted to politics by ordinary human pleasures. What, then, does attract them?

To answer this question, we have interviewed politicians in an attempt to learn about the satisfactions they get from political life. We have conducted these interviews in many settings, both in the United States and abroad. Among the groups we have studied are Connecticut state legislators, Virginia city councilmen, Pennsylvania party leaders, Maine city councilmen, District of Columbia councilmen, French deputies, Colombian politicians, political leaders in the Dominican Republic, Austrian legislators, and Venezuelan congressmen. In addition, we have added a number of isolated interviews with individuals ranging from a New Hampshire senatorial candidate to a San Diego city councilman. We have, further, examined a number of interviews made available to us by our colleagues, and we have studied many autobiographies by politicians.

As a result of these explorations, we found it necessary to modify some of our original conceptions about the motivation of politicians. There is a natural tendency—which we shared—to approach the motivation issue by looking for specific goals, reasons, or purposes. Thus, we are disposed to say that A is in politics "to help poor people," or that B is in politics "to promote the peaceful use of atomic energy." Empirically, when one actually gets a close look at politicians, the proposition that they participate for intellectual "reasons" or to carry out some specific goal simply will not stand up.

Many politicians will themselves explicitly downgrade or discard "reasons" to account for their participation, pointing instead to their "personality" (e.g., "it's in my nature"). When asked specifically "Why are you in politics?" politicians rarely answer (in a personal, private interview) by giving a specific policy goal or reason. Many of them are frankly puzzled about their motivation.

Furthermore, a goal interpretation of motivation would predict that a politician would retire from politics when the specific purpose is accomplished. This prediction will typically prove to be inaccurate; accomplishment of a given goal is not accompanied by withdrawal from political life.

None of the foregoing should be taken to mean that politicians do not have goals and purposes. They each have, like the rest of us, a multitude of aims, both public and personal. But these specific purposes, we came to realize, do not convincingly account for their participation.

Instead, we discovered, it was an emotional type of drive that propelled individuals to accept the rigors of political life. In some politicians, this drive can fairly be called a compulsion — an unreasoning, even self-destructive, impulse that resembles an addiction. But the term "compulsion" overstates the nature of this drive for most politicians. True, the drive is emotional, not rational, and it is salient. But it is not self-destructive or uncontrollable. Most politicians we have encountered are as healthy and well adjusted as the rest of us; but they do differ from most nonpoliticians in having a particular, quasi-compulsive drive. To refer to this emotional need we use the term "incentive."

As we looked more closely at incentives, studying politicians in an effort to identify the emotional needs that motivated them, we reached two conclusions. First, there are a number of quite distinct incentives; and second, politicians tend to have only one or another of these incentives.

The first point should not, perhaps, come as a surprise. Nevertheless, there is sometimes a tendency to suppose that politicians are "all alike," that they form a homogeneous class. This view is perhaps understandable for those whose knowledge of politicians is based on media presentation, for the media impose a uniform, formalistic context in portraying politicians. One could watch dozens of sessions of *Face the Nation* and never suppose that the drive of one guest was significantly different from another — or, for that matter, that any guest had any drive whatsoever. But for anyone who has known a number of politicians personally, it is readily apparent that dramatically different types of individuals are found in politics. These fundamental differences make plausible the contention that different incentives exist among politicians.

The second point is somewhat more difficult to accept. It is our usual presumption that motivation is complex, that human beings are always characterized by a multiplicity of motives and drives. This was our assumption at the outset of our research. And, of course, we are not offering the conclusion that politicians are simple to understand. Each politician represents a unique configuration of beliefs, habits, abilities, traits, purposes, and so forth. The idea that any person, politicians included, will fit entirely into a single category for all purposes is to us quite preposterous.

Incentives, however, treat only one aspect of an individual: the emotional drive that accounts for participation in politics. Our point is therefore limited to this issue: each politician (with few exceptions) has only one incentive, not a mixture of incentives.

Part of the difficulty in accepting this conclusion comes from a tendency to project observations about people in general to politicians. We observe that most of our friends and neighbors exhibit a mixture of drives—a little of this impulse, a certain amount of that drive, and so on. But politicians are not a representative sample of human beings. The role, as we have pointed out, is stressful and taxing; these demands select out of the general run of humanity only those individuals with drives strong enough to counterbalance the sacrifices. Our typical friends and neighbors, with their mixture of weak drives, do not enter politics—or, if they do, their participation tends to be marginal or transitory. Politicians are, motivationally, a special class of individuals; therefore, we should not expect observations about the motivation of nonpoliticians to apply to them.

The conclusion that politicians have single incentives is, for us, an empirical one; we reached it from the study of the interviews themselves. An incentive is not, of course, directly observable. One infers incentives from what the individual says in the interview. An interview aimed at disclosing incentives is personally focused. The respondent is encouraged to talk about his areas of interest, his satisfactions and frustrations, his personal view of others, his private and political philosophy, and so on. From this material one infers the emotional need that has given rise to these interests and perspectives.

Most interviews are remarkable in being highly homogeneous. That is, the many different elements are consistent with a single drive. If the topics the respondent chooses to talk about indicate incentive A, for example, then the frustrations noted will indicate incentive A, the manner of evaluating others will reflect incentive A, striking features of the respondent's personal philosophy will reflect incentive A, and so on. Indeed, the coherent character of an interview is often detected by the interviewer before he can identify the basis of the consistency. Several of us have had field experiences of this type. Upon interviewing a politician, we sensed from the homogeneous, reiterative texture of the interview that he had a specific incentive, but we could not identify that incentive until later analysis. It is this coherence of the typical interview that leads us to conclude that politicians usually have a single incentive. We have encountered very few interviews in which the material clearly suggests a number of incentives.

We do find some interviews where the responses and discussion are neutral, not suggesting any particular emotional drive. These respondents, it seems, have weak incentives, or, perhaps, they have no incentive. Following the proposition that more strongly motivated individuals will be found in the more demanding roles, we would expect that those individuals without incentives would appear in more marginal, less taxing roles. This has been our experience. We find that as one moves to lower-level political offices, cases of individuals with no clear incentive occur more frequently. However, even at the local level, most politicians do have an identifiable incentive.

The specific incentives we have encountered are the following:

1. Status—the need for prestige or public recognition;
2. Program—the need to work upon specific, concrete public policy issues;
3. Conviviality—the need to please others and gain their approval;
4. Obligation—the need to follow one's conscience, to engage in morally correct behavior;
5. Game—the need to compete with others in structured, intellectually challenging interactions;
6. Mission*—the need to be that committed to a transcendental cause that gives meaning and purpose to life;
7. Adulation*—the need for exaggerated praise and affection.

These brief definitions are, of necessity, incomplete and might easily mislead; the reader is urged to examine the full descriptions of each type in the following chapters.

It should be emphasized that these incentive types were not arbitrarily proposed at the outset of our research. They are based on what the actual interviews suggested to us. The process of discovering the different incentive types—which took place in the period 1964-1969—was an empirical one. We would encounter one interview that had the particular coherent or patterned quality discussed above. In the course of further interviewing, we would encounter other politicians with strikingly similar orientations. In some cases, the members of this

---

*The mission and adulation incentives have been encountered almost entirely in foreign settings. Since they occur rarely among American politicians, we shall deal with them only briefly in this book.

type would duplicate each other's thoughts, even to the extent of using the same imagery or the same analogies. This congruence was especially remarkable when it occurred between politicians of different cultures and countries.

In this way, we came to realize that there were distinct types of politicians. It was only a short step to move from the recognition of these coherent types to postulating that they each spring from a particular emotional need. This formulation greatly simplifies the categories. The emotional need is seen as the root cause or ordering force for each type. It explains the cluster of characteristics. Furthermore, defining the types in terms of their emotional needs, or incentives, gives energy and direction to the typology. It opens the door to a predictive theory of political behavior based on this axiom: a politician tends to behave in a manner consistent with his incentive.

The initial identification of the incentive types has been followed by a period, still continuing, of interviewing and classifying more politicians. We find that the incentive types stand up: we can place most respondents in these categories. We have not encountered any additional incentive types — although we always keep a lookout in this direction.

At the same time, we have been using our incentive findings to analyze the behavior of politicians in different systems. As we shall explain in the concluding chapter, a knowledge of incentives provides a useful basis for understanding many features of politics, both in the United States and abroad.

Many of the foregoing observations about the motivation of politicians are novel; they represent discoveries. Although they may seem vaguely familiar, the incentive types, with all their interrelated characteristics, are not generally known. We certainly did not know about them before we undertook our research.

It may seem surprising that this gap should exist in the popular understanding about the motivation of politicians, since almost everyone has considerable familiarity with politicians. Their statements of preference and purpose daily fill the airwaves and newspapers. Political scientists are constantly studying politicians. Philosophers speculate about them and novelists depict them. Given this wealth of commentary and information, why isn't the incentive dimension generally recognized?

The answer, we believe, is that incentive findings emerge from studying politicians in a manner not normally attempted. To get at the incentive aspect requires informal, personally focused, open-ended interviews with a number of politicians. The information the general public receives about politicians is not of this type. It is therefore not useful for making one aware of the emotional basis of participation, or for identifying the specific drives involved. Many barriers, biases, and circumstances operate to prevent incentive-relevant material from entering the stream of what we learn about politicians.

1. *The stress on information.* Politicians are viewed mainly as sources of information. When reporters interview a politician, it is typically to obtain information about his policy positions and his intended decisions. Will he report the bill from committee? Will he vote for the treaty? Does he intend to seek the nomination? None of these questions will shed light on incentives. They are not personally focused; they do not probe the respondent's interests, satisfactions, and frustrations.

Occasionally a personally focused question is asked by a reporter—in a TV interview, let us say. But in this highly public context, the answer is likely to be formal and superficial. The same point applies to speeches: these are public, purposeful utterances that do not normally reflect the emotional need of the speaker. Autobiographies, too, often suffer from this problem. Sometimes they are frank and personally focused, and, as we shall see in the following chapters, quite useful for the purposes of incentive analysis. But most autobiographies are quite formal and distant, revealing little about the writer himself.

Our friends and colleagues occasionally ask us for our opinion about the incentive of this or that prominent politician. In most cases, we have to confess to not having an opinion: the flow of information from the mass media is simply an insufficient basis on which to speculate.

In recent years, political scientists have also taken to interviewing politicians, but here too the stress is normally upon information: How is the committee agenda set? Who usually initiates proposals? What campaign technique appeared to be most successful? Several of the authors of this book, prior to becoming aware of incentives, conducted informational-type interviewing. We find, in retrospect, that these interviews are not generally useful for detecting incentives. They were aimed at exploring certain areas of fact and ignored the personal dimension.

Politicians are typically viewed as sources of news and information. Perhaps this orientation reflects the degree to which we take them for granted. A politician might legitimately complain: "Why aren't they interested in me as a person, as a human being who gets frustrated, bored, anxious, upset, delighted, fulfilled?" Of course, it is true that many politicians do not go out of their way to reveal their full personalities to us. In any case, unless we do get interested in politicians as people, we shall miss the incentive aspect.

2. *The emphasis on evaluation.* Politicians arouse strong reactions. The dominant feature in most thinking and discourse about a politician is evaluative: do we like or dislike him? Our likes and dislikes, in turn, are shaped by our image of his apparent policy goals. In the popular mind, it is difficult to separate the evaluation of a politician's policy goals from his motivation. Politicians with good goals, it is assumed, have

good or noble motives; politicians with wrong or silly goals have unworthy or sinister motives. This popular orientation forecloses the treatment of motives as an independent, researchable category. Judgments about a politician's motives are simply an extension of the observer's evaluation of his policy aims.

To perceive incentives, one must set aside the evaluative orientation. One must stop thinking in terms of likes and dislikes and look for emotional needs. There is no certain correspondence between any of these needs and a particular policy goal. Politicians with the same incentive may easily be found on opposite sides of any issue. The observer who ascribes motives to politicians on the basis of his reaction to their apparent policy aims will end up with a shallow and misleading typology.

Furthermore, if we like or dislike a politician before we attempt to study his motivation, there will usually be a tendency to shape our conclusions accordingly. This point argues against attempting to reach conclusions about political motivation by treating the prominent politicians of the day, such as presidents and presidential candidates. But it is precisely these politicians whose motives are most widely discussed. The result is easy to see. Popular conclusions about motivation are simply projections of the observer's preferences. Politicians liked are said to be motivated by "idealism"; those disliked are "opportunists," and so on. Such categories are the outgrowth of the popular need to express approval or disapproval in different words, not the result of an empirical examination of politicians up close.

3. *The reliance on single cases.* The recognition of incentive types is possible only if one closely examines a number of personally focused interviews. The study of a single politician, no matter how detailed and thorough, will not lead to this recognition. Every politician will exhibit attitudes and perspectives falling into three different categories: (1) idiosyncratic features — unique to a given politician; (2) cultural or role features — com-

mon to most politicians similarly located; and (3) incentive-related features—characteristic of a particular type of politician. Until one has examined a number of politicians, it is not possible to separate this third category of material from the others.

Could anyone ever detect the existence of a tree species from the examination, however close, of one tree? Each tree represents a combination of (1) unique features, (2) features common to most trees in the area, and (3) species characteristics. The leaves are mottled, for example: Perhaps this is a species characteristic, or perhaps it is a disease unique to this particular tree. The trunk is not strictly vertical—is this a species characteristic or the result of local wind or soil conditions? Such questions cannot be answered unless a number of cases are examined.

The close examinations of politicians that have been made usually have been single-case analyses. Therefore, they could not be expected to uncover the incentive dimension. Biographers, for example, usually study one man minutely—a perspective that does not encourage the separation of the idiosyncratic from the recurrent. A similar problem exists for those who work for, or otherwise get close to, a single politician. The incentive dimension is unlikely to be perceived in this one individual, being mixed with idiosyncratic and role-influenced features.

4. *The a priori impulse.* Our culture transmits to us a considerable body of assumptions about motivational types of politicians. This background of assumptions will typically form the basis of both research on politicians and the evaluation of the research of others. But should it? To what extent is this cultural heritage grounded upon sustained, objective empirical examination?

We have already noted that many popular typological terms —idealistic, opportunistic, power hungry, humanitarian, and so on—owe their origin to no specific research, but are thinly disguised substitutes for evaluative terms.

Novelists and movie writers contribute views of political motivation. Where do they get them? An occasional writer may have undertaken a close and systematic examination of politicians, but in most cases the writer creates his characters from the same sources available to the rest of us: newspapers, TV, movies, biographies, self-analysis. Dramatic requirements—for tension, for plot, for good guys and bad guys, for a fitting ending—further detract from accuracy.

Philosophers, too, have offered views of political motives. Again, a rare few may have an empirical basis for their observations. But in most cases, philosophers have not been interested in describing reality, but in constructing overarching generalizations and in prescribing ideal behavior. Political typologies are invented to serve these schemes. For example, Aristotle divides politicians into two classes: those who rule in their own interest and those who rule in the interest of all. The dichotomy—quite unworkable empirically—is required by an abstract theory of governmental forms.

Our cultural heritage on the subject of political motivation is extensive, but it rests upon dubious foundations. It is not a satisfactory starting point for research. The scholar who seeks to detect political types would do best if he put aside all that he thought he knew and simply interviewed a number of politicians and then began generalizing on the basis of what he had seen.

Unfortunately, the a priori impulse hangs heavily upon the intellectual community. Few scholars have actually given themselves the chance to discover something about politicians—such as incentives. The pattern of research that is typically followed is to start with a model or conception drawn from a philosopher or from one's own imagination (i.e., from the diffuse cultural heritage), set forth hypotheses to be tested, and devise interviews and questionnaires—all before one goes into the field.

Such practices have their explanations. Group research requires the road to be mapped in advance. Grants are difficult to obtain without a fully constructed research design. Doctoral students often come to grief if they set out on their own. Research appears more scholarly and more acceptable if it is "based on the literature."

Another condition favoring a priorism in research is the emphasis on quantitative measurements. For a variety of reasons, some good and some bad, academic social science today favors quantitative data. In order to obtain such data, the researcher must devise specific measurement procedures at the outset of research. In devising these measures, researchers are unavoidably guided by the prevailing a priori speculations about the way the world is. The push for quantitative data, then, discourages scholars from having an exploratory "look-see" and tends to restrict them to counting what is already supposed to exist.

Regardless of the explanation, the a priori approach will preclude the detection of the incentive variable. That is, one reason why incentives have not been noticed more is that most researchers are looking for something else.

The importance of this point is suggested by the results obtained when an open, exploratory approach to the study of politicians has been adopted. Researchers following this approach have, in several cases, uncovered types corresponding to the incentive categories.

One of the first such studies was done by Aaron Wildavsky on delegates to the 1964 Republican convention.[1] The research originally focused on the theme of decision making under uncertainty; interviewers were directed to ask questions probing this subject. It quickly became clear that the outcome of this convention was a foregone conclusion and that there was little uncertainty to study. The emphasis of the research was therefore shifted to an open-ended exploration of the delegates themselves. It was noticed that a number of Goldwater supporters contrasted markedly with other delegates in being unusually preoccupied with proper conduct, with the shoulds and oughts of politics. They adopted the view that "it's better to be right than to win in politics." These participants were dubbed "purists"; they correspond to the obligation type we have observed.

Another study of a flexible, exploratory nature is James David Barber's examination of freshman state representatives in Connecticut.[2] Barber initially divided his subjects into four categories based on their standing on two simple variables (stated expectation of returning and activity in the legislature). He then conducted personally focused interviews with some of the respondents in each category. From these interviews Barber abstracted several distinct types, which again correspond to the incentive types we have observed: advertiser (status), lawmaker (program), and spectator (conviviality).[3]

A recent study by Michael Maccoby further encourages us to believe that exploratory, personally focused research will encounter the incentive dimension.[4] Maccoby did not study politicians; he interviewed corporation executives. There would be an expectation of finding the incentive types in this setting, however, for many executive positions are similar to political ones: they are personally taxing and require considerable effort to obtain. Maccoby found that he could divide his interview respondents into four types, each of which seems to correspond to an incentive type we have encountered: the craftsman (program), the company man (conviviality), the gamesman (game), and the jungle fighter (status).

The incentive types, then, appear to have been detected by other researchers who have used an open, exploratory approach. We are confident that if others look for them in the appropriate way, free from the various problems noted above, they also will observe them.

2 The Status Incentive

THE NEED TO BE somebody is a common human longing. To be recognized by strangers, to have one's name appear in print, to be held in awe: human beings seem to be gratified by such experiences. Most cultures, to varying degrees, encourage this impulse for status. Young men are enjoined to be ambitious, to amount to something. To become a "distinguished" lawyer, scholar, doctor, or whatever is judged a fitting goal. We erect monuments for and name boulevards after those who have become famous; in this way we reward and encourage the pursuit of fame.

Though almost everyone has some need for status, the strength of this need varies. For most persons it is too weak to cause excessive efforts to gratify it. For others, however, the status need is strong; it is an omnipresent anxiety about being highly regarded.

For such people, politics is an attractive terrain, for scarcely any other undertaking offers such abundant status rewards. Politicians' names fill our newspapers and our history books. Their faces dominate our television screens. Onlookers struggle with each other to touch the hand of the passing president; tourists gape in awe at a senator eating a fruit salad in the Capitol restaurant. Politicians are always in demand on the lecture circuit and in the center of attention at cocktail parties. It is not surprising, then, that one of the most common incentives propelling individuals into politics is the need for status.

In presenting each of the incentive types in this book, we have chosen to examine two political figures who illustrate each type. In the first example, we shall analyze an interview; in the second, we shall analyze an autobiography. This mode of presentation departs somewhat from our usual method, which is to give excerpts from a wide variety of interviews to stress the universality of each type. We feel, however, that focusing on specific individuals makes the presentation easier to follow and more lifelike. It should be stressed, though, that the individuals are selected and analyzed as representative of an incentive type. Therefore, their idiosyncratic characteristics—which would properly interest historians, psychoanalysts, or biographers—will be overlooked in the interest of highlighting the representative, incentive-relevant features.

How is the status incentive recognized? As we explained in the preceding chapter, this question cannot be answered from a distance. We must study the personally focused commentary of the politician himself. Using such material, we can detect an incentive by inference from the topics the politician chooses to talk about and from his perspectives on those topics. The politician's particular emotional need, or incentive, governs his interests and perspectives; one can, therefore, reason backward from the interests and perspectives exhibited in the interview to the emotional need that underlies them.

In the case of the status incentive, we find that the topics, attitudes, and perspectives exhibited in the interview reflect a preoccupation with status. The politician stresses his public recognition; he raises topics involving personal advancement; his attention focuses on the publicity associated with a subject; he makes evaluations from a status frame of reference; his explanations of the behavior of others assume that the drive for high standing underlies their purposes.

To illustrate this process of inferring incentives, let us turn to the examination of two politicians with a status incentive.

I. DAVID CLARK: "LIKE BEING AVIS"

David Clark is a councilman, a Democrat, in the large Virginia city of Culver.* He is rather short, thin, and, at age forty-one, still boyish looking. Having received the highest vote in the council race, as he takes care to explain, he is also vice mayor of the city. He describes himself as working "seven days a week" in his council job. Why does he do it? In the interview with him, he is asked this question in several ways. Early in the interview, the conversation drifts toward his first activity in politics, his working for John F. Kennedy in the 1960 presidential election. The interviewer then asks about his reason for running for the council:

> Q: And then, like for council, what sort of made you decide to run?
>
> CLARK: Well, I was on two or three committees. In fact I was on four council committees. Several of them I did real well with. I was named Culver's Outstanding Young Man one year—'65. In '66 I got named by a national panel of...one of the Outstanding Young Men of America.
>
> Q: Boy!
>
> CLARK: In '67, building up, I got named one of the outstanding, one of the nation's outstanding civic leaders.
>
> Q: That's wonderful.
>
> CLARK: So that's '65, '66, '67. Then I ran [for council] in '68, so that this...I stepped out real well.

Notice that Clark does not answer the question directly. He is asked for reasons for his seeking a council post; he answers by recounting a historical sequence. But, indirectly, he is answering the question. What topic is he dwelling upon? What is his frame of reference? Did he do "real well" in the sense of discharging an obligation, or in the sense of getting a program

---

*The respondent's name and city have been changed to protect his identity.

underway? Apparently not. For Clark, doing "real well" is being named Outstanding Young Man of America; it is to have "stepped out real well." Significantly, nowhere in the interview does he mention the subject matter or purposes of those committees he did "real well with." Our inference—and in this case it is transparently obvious—is that Clark is preoccupied with recognition; he has a status incentive.

Somewhat later in the interview Clark makes a similarly transparent comment:

> Q: I was going to ask, would you like to go on being a councilman?
> CLARK: Well, to be honest about it, being the vice mayor is... it pushes you into a position that there's only one thing you can do. Like being Avis. If you want to be number one... (trails off)
> Q: So you want to run for mayor?
> CLARK: I'd either run for mayor or quit.

What is the perspective that underlies Clark's view? What, for him, is the purpose of politics? It is manifestly false that being vice mayor means "that there's *only one thing* you can do." After all, one could go on being vice mayor for the rest of one's life. Clark's remark is true only if one supposes that the purpose of political activity is to rise upward, to enhance one's standing. Apparently this is Clark's orientation. Again, inference leads us to the conclusion that Clark is oriented toward status.

Comments as transparent as these are rare in interviews with status types. Clark is a particularly unsophisticated respondent with an almost childlike presumption that status success is valued by everyone. Most status types are less forthcoming on themes of success and ambition; the interpretation of their remarks requires more care.

An illustration of a more typical status remark is the continuation of the preceding excerpt. Clark had been asked if he would like to continue as councilman, with the answer reported above. Then the questioner continues:

Q: What about other offices—the Assembly or Congress?

CLARK: Oh, I like the General Assembly. But I like the local problems; there's not too many people take time out to take care of them. There's a lot of prestige, a lot of position being in the House of Delegates or a state senator. But it's not my cup of tea. I like the local problems. They go on seven days a week. I wouldn't mind taking care of maybe another four years of it.

Q: Well, it seems with your sort of energy and drive that you can go very far.

CLARK: Well, you've got to be self... I'm self-satisfied about things. I just don't have any ambition to being a state man, although I'm very fortunate.... Most of your better committee chairmen are members of the House and Senate who are in a good position. I generally, I know them. And I associate with them when I go to Richmond "Urban Twelve." I'm on their, I'm on their executive committee. In fact, I'm the only vice mayor of the whole group. The rest of them are mayors. But... I'm not, I just don't have the ambition about it. I like local problems. And somebody has to do it. It's hard to get people to take care of local things.

Q: Yeah, I know.

CLARK: Everybody wants to run down to Richmond, be a member of the House, a member of the Senate. They show up every so often; then you go on a committee, you meet every so often. But local government in my book is seven days a week.

One might interpret this passage to imply that Clark does not have a status incentive. After all, he renounces an ambition for higher office; surely this appears to be a conclusive denial of a status orientation.

Let us remind ourselves, however, of the method whereby incentives are detected. We do not accept at face value statements the interview respondent may make about his motives. When Clark says that he is unambitious, we suspend judgment on the point. What we are looking for are the topics dwelt upon and the perspective the respondent adopts toward these topics.

An inspection of Clark's comments on the state legislature repeatedly reveals a status preoccupation. First, he elevates his own importance and disparages others: others don't "take time out" to take care of local problems—as he does. Then he mentions the "prestige" of being in the Assembly. Then he stresses his association with high-status individuals and pointedly notes his holding of high position. He then returns to boosting his self-image and disparaging others. He also imputes to others a status-seeking orientation: they want to "run down to Richmond." The self-projection here is quite clear, for Clark himself had just digressed to note that he, too, runs down to Richmond. The proper interpretation of this comment, then, is that it consistently displays a status orientation.

Clark's true intention about running for the General Assembly is a separate problem. It is important to separate the meaning of "ambition" as a diffuse need—the status incentive—from more specific intentions of running for a particular office. Specific intentions are governed by many things in addition to incentives: opportunities, likelihood of success, family or job responsibilities, financial position, and so on. It is perfectly possible for a status-incentive politician to have no intention of seeking another office.

It is clear that Clark is ambitious in the diffuse sense. Indeed, his aversion to being "number two" dramatically contradicts the claim that he is "self-satisfied." It is entirely possible, however, that he does not intend to seek an Assembly position. Perhaps his way is blocked by a strong, popular incumbent, perhaps his employment prevents him leaving town for extended periods of time, or whatever.

Inspection of another comment, again more typical of what one will encounter in an interview with a status type, further illustrates the importance of inference as opposed to the direct acceptance of what is said:

> Q: What quality do you think is most important for a person to succeed in politics?

CLARK: Sincerity. He can snow people, he can give them the... pass the buck on the phone. He can do the same thing at council meetings. But I think that being sincere is the most important asset that any councilman, that any guy wanting to be a councilman, can have. You can't snow people around here.

At first glance, this remark suggests an obligation orientation: a preoccupation with integrity and honesty, with doing the right thing. But there is an important difference in perspective. For the obligation-incentive type, sincerity (or honesty) is intrinsically desirable. Politicians ought to be honest because it is the right way to behave, not because it is expedient. Indeed, obligation types believe that honesty is inexpedient politically; sincerity and frankness are cherished precisely because they must be upheld in opposition to one's political interests.

This is not Clark's perspective. For him, sincerity is an "asset," something that aids one in getting ahead. It is expedient because "you can't snow people around here." From Clark's perspective, if you could "snow people," then sincerity would have no defense. Even in the discussion of moral virtues, then, we find Clark's status incentive, his orientation toward advancement and success, governing his perspective. It is not the virtue he identifies that sets him apart from other politicians; what is distinctive is the calculating perspective from which he views this virtue.

In the preceding pages we have examined specific comments. What of the interview as a whole? What is revealed by the topics stressed and the topics ignored?

One topic that was largely ignored was substantive policy issues. Naturally, the conversation touched upon many policy questions, but at no point did Clark go into any detail. In spite of probes by the interviewer, Clark's comments on policy matters were confined to general, superficial observations. The following is typical:

Q: Locally, in your last campaign, what kind of issues were there?

CLARK: Well, I ran on three things. I had a program. I carried most of it out. I ran on three things: promoting the city's assets, developing its potential, correcting its shortcomings. That's the platform I ran on. (pause)

Q: Uh huh. You said you carried...which things have you carried out?

CLARK: Well, I've been tied up in the River Drive. It's gone real well. In industrial development, we built, we financed a new sort of industrial commission in the city council. Quality education, we certainly think we've got that. That was one of my main goals. I'm a great supporter of the police department, upgrading the qualifications. We set up a police academy here.

Q: Oh really?

CLARK: And I've gone about buying a building to give the police department its own identity. And I came up with a recommendation to hire thirty-three additional policemen. They made it. So most of the things I ran on — I've been very lucky — have come out.

Notice how Clark glosses over all the trade-offs, analyses, value conflicts, and concrete details inherent in policy questions. For him, policies are neatly wrapped "accomplishments." The substance of policy questions does not interest him; he focuses upon his connection with these matters, his proposals and his accomplishments. There is, too, a certain glib, mechanical quality to this recital that makes it sound like a television commercial in an election campaign.

From the absence of penetrating policy discussion in the interview, we infer that Clark's main interest is not in policy or policy making. This lack of interest in substantive policy making is a characteristic of status types; but it is also characteristic of several other incentive types. Hence, it is merely consistent with Clark's hypothesized status incentive; it does not point specifically to that incentive alone. The other aspects of his treatment of policy — the stress on self and the effort to create an impressive appearance of policy command—are more specifically characteristic of status types.

Clark does not have anything penetrating to say about policy in the interview. On other topics—the Democratic presidential primary race, the mood of the voters, the attractions of the city of Culver—he is similarly lacking in insight and enthusiasm. Clark, it appears, is not a particularly thoughtful or articulate individual. But there is one point in the interview where he opens up, talking more freely, becoming more analytical and more specific. The subject is campaign techniques. The interviewer has been asking about various publicity devices, such as billboards and bumper stickers. Then Clark himself volunteers the following comment:

> CLARK: I like using matches.
> Q: Matchbooks?
> CLARK: Right. You can stand on every corner.... I like using matchbooks really better over everything. I'll tell you why. Because a lot of politicians will give out cards with their name on them—standing at the bus stop, for instance, or the shopping center—and maybe 30 or 40 percent of the people really don't care, and they throw them down. Then comes another guy along behind and sees them laying on the ground after you are gone: "He threw his propaganda down and people really don't want him." Well a match, a good book of matches, I don't care whether you're female or male or what, you stick it in your pocketbook or you stick it in your shirt pocket.
> Q: You don't throw it away.
> CLARK: You don't throw a book of matches down.
> Q: That's good.
> CLARK: So, I think the best thing that a guy—in my case, I believe in book matches.
> Q: Yeah. I guess they're not too expensive either?
> CLARK: No, they're not. Twenty-five dollars for a couple thousand books, which is not bad at all.
> Q: Yes.

CLARK: Everybody takes a match home. You hand it to some lady at the shopping center. If she doesn't smoke, she's not going to throw it down. She's going to throw it in the front seat of the car, and her husband drives it the next day, and he'll use it. Or she'll stick it in her pocketbook. At the bridge club, somebody wants a match, and she'll pull one out. I don't believe in *ever* giving out your name on cards.

Compared to the dull, superficial character of the rest of the interview, this comment is remarkably vivid. This point is highly significant.

Each incentive leads to an interest in a particular phase of politics and, hence, to a disposition to converse about that phase. Program types want to talk about policies; conviviality types want to talk about people and experiences of friendship; game types dwell upon competitive interactions; obligation types focus on issues of right and wrong. In each case, the incentive supplies a "natural" topic of conversation, something the individual has thought much about and which interests him.

The natural topic of conversation for the status type is the subject, personally focused, of obtaining positions. A status participant is, after all, interested in his own political success. It is natural that this will be a topic he thinks much about and about which he has developed some insights. This interest may take the form of a discussion of the strategy and tactics used by the politician, or a history of a past struggle for a position. If rapport is good, the subject may dwell at length on his plans and calculations for his future career. When such topics stand out in an interview—as with David Clark's discussion of his publicity technique—this emphasis indicates a status incentive.

Another general feature that characterizes interviews with status types is the frequent reference to the status aspect of people, institutions, and experiences. A sampling of such references from the Clark interview includes the following:

I'm working for Culver's biggest industry.

Culver is the Governor's home town.

I got associated with John Kennedy in 1959.

I moved up to President of the Young Democrats.

In anything—politics or anything else—you got to have a rub-off or an image. And I have a real good one.

I've traveled all over the country.

I met Eugene McCarthy here in Culver.

Muskie is close to environmental quality, and I'm on a national committee for that myself—the National League of Cities.

I work for a big company, and I can adjust my schedule to taking care of these people.

My Great-uncle John was...the first mayor of Culver.

None of these comments, taken separately, would have much significance; together they reveal a preoccupation with recognition and social importance. They indicate that Clark is looking at the world from the perspective of a man preoccupied with status.

An inspection of the interview with David Clark, then, keeps returning us to the same conclusion: status is the emotional need ordering his interests and perspectives. In a sense, a personally focused interview of this kind is like a hologram: the entire interview as well as each part of it carries the same picture. The interview has a coherent texture with each comment revealing the same underlying perspective.

The hologram analogy is overdrawn, however, for most interviews do not consist of purely incentive-relevant material. There generally is, in addition, a considerable amount of what might be called neutral conversation. For example, approximately one third of the Clark interview should be classified as neutral material, that is, comments that reveal nothing about incentives one way or the other. Such neutral discussion is recognizable as comments commonly found in interviews with many politicians.

As an aid to singling out incentive-relevant comments, we have put in Appendix I a capsule summary of the characteristics typically exhibited in interviews with each incentive type. In these summaries, we have noted the main themes and attitudes relevant for the detection of each type.

II. William Jennings Bryan: "The Lure of the College Prize"

Autobiographies by politicians are not generally useful for incentive analysis. Normally the autobiographer conceives his task as that of recounting the facts of his life history and the people and events surrounding that history. As a result, the personal preoccupations of the writer are largely ignored. One has, in effect, a biography of the traditional sort.

Occasionally, an autobiography departs from this model. The author does not play the role of historian; instead, he expresses himself. He reveals his likes and dislikes and his private reactions to people and events. The result is a personally focused account reflecting the interests and preoccupations of the writer.

Such personally focused autobiographies have several characteristics. First, they depart from chronological presentation—beyond a general drift. Many points are raised out of chronological order; substantial gaps in the life history occur. Second, the work is apparently written from memory, without significant use of notes or files. The author is uninterested in producing a scholarly work or historical record; instead, he expresses what is on his mind. Finally, these personally focused autobiographies exhibit a highly idiosyncratic choice of topics and themes. Major historical events that readers would be interested in are ignored, while insignificant happenings are dwelt upon at length. Instead of emphasizing what readers might think is important, the author employs his personal standards of importance.

It is difficult to say when or why such a personally focused autobiography would be written. Whatever the explanation, it is clear that when we do encounter this kind of autobiography, it will be useful for incentive determination. It resembles the personally focused interview in reflecting the interests and preoccupations of the subject himself. One such autobiography, to which we now turn, is that written by William Jennings Bryan.[1]

Bryan is popularly referred to as an "idealist." He stands out in American history as one of the clearest examples of this "type" of politician. From this image, one might suppose that his incentive was obligation, or perhaps program or mission. We are totally unprepared to discover, upon inspecting his autobiography, that Bryan had a status incentive.

To a considerable extent, our error traces to our dependence upon a faulty vocabulary and misleading conceptions of political types. In this case, it is the term "idealist" that misleads us.

We tend to apply the term "idealist" to a politician who is a highly visible, vocal position taker. Bryan was clearly that. He is perhaps best remembered for his stand on the free coinage of silver and his "cross of gold" speech. But he vigorously advocated many other measures: workers' rights, women's rights, direct election of senators, prohibition of child labor, the progressive income tax, regulation of business, anti-imperialism, and "peace." Deviating from Bryan's otherwise "liberal" record are his positions, also stridently advocated, in favor of prohibition and against the teaching of evolution in public schools.

Bryan also conforms to the notion of an idealist as one who —through his ideas may be accepted—enjoys little personal political success. After two terms in the House of Representatives from Nebraska (1891-1895), he unsuccessfully sought a Senate seat (1895), and three times ran unsuccessfully as the Democratic presidential nominee (1896, 1900, 1908). He was made secretary of state by Woodrow Wilson in 1913—a post he resigned only two years later.

Thus, Bryan conforms to what might be called a behavioral definition of an "idealist": a vocal, visible, out-of-power position taker. If the term were confined only to this aspect, it might serve a useful purpose. Unfortunately, there is another aspect of the term that amounts to a motivational definition: an idealist is one who is deeply preoccupied with the substance of the measures he advocates and whose desire to see these measures enacted motivates his political participation. In popular usage, these two meanings fuse inseparably in the term "idealist": vigorous position takers, it is presumed, must be motivated by their policy preoccupations. This presumption leads to the expectation that Bryan must have been deeply interested in the measures he advocated and that this deep interest motivated his political activity. An inspection of the autobiography readily contradicts this conclusion. It illustrates the danger of relying upon the popular images of politicians and exposes the inadequacy of the popular terms by which we categorize them.

The focus of Bryan's autobiography is clearly established in the opening lines of the preface:

> In giving the public the story of my life I trust I may be credited with something more than a desire to acquaint the public with myself. The time has passed when I could have any ulterior motive in a heart-to-heart talk with the American people. Whatever ambition I have had has been more than gratified; I feel that I have received more than I have deserved and been abundantly repaid for the efforts I have made in behalf of the American people.

> It is my purpose to show that in my own case good fortune has had more to do with such success as I may have achieved than any efforts of my own. Success in politics—and, to a large extent in other lines of activity—is the conjunction of opportunity and the preparedness to meet it. (P. 9)

Bryan focuses upon himself and drifts immediately toward the subjects of "ambition" and "success." The defensive tone is particularly revealing. It indicates that Bryan is preoccupied with self-glorification, a case of protesting too much. A man unconcerned with status does not worry that he might be accused of status-seeking by writing his autobiography; he would not begin his autobiography by defending himself against such a charge. After all, readers might expect the purpose of an autobiography to be anything: to entertain, to instruct, to inform. That readers will presume self-glorification to be the purpose of the book, then, reflects a projection on Bryan's part. It is his preoccupation with self-glorification, it would seem, that leads him to assume that readers will be similarly preoccupied.

Indeed, the entire preface, in which Bryan attempts to strike a self-effacing posture, is profoundly contradictory. A page later, he writes as follows:

> In politics as in the army, the generals receive the glory while the enlisted men die in the trenches. The names that are prominent become household words, while the multitude who bear the burden are nameless in history.
>
> That which was called Bryanism in derision by many, represented a group of substantial reforms; it was not an individual thing but rather the result of united effort of some six and half millions of American voters. I was but one of the millions, but because I was in a position of leadership I received the glory and the censure, while others equally earnest and often with more sacrifice labored and died unknown to fame. (P. 10)

What a curious choice of words with which to efface one's self! Bryan is the "general" getting "glory." His name is the household word. That Bryan should focus on "glory" (and not upon policy accomplishment) as the reward to be distributed in politics further reveals the center of his attention. Notice also how he inserts "and the censure" in the last sentence. This phrase is a digression that contradicts the logical structure of the sentence (I had the good, they had the bad). Its insertion reveals an undue sensitivity to criticism on the part of the author: he could not resist mentioning the censure aspect.

Most noticeable on the self-effacement theme in the preface is Bryan's explicitly stated intention, made on the first page, "to shift the accent from 'I' to 'they' as to purge my Memoirs of every trace of egotism or self-assertion" (p. 9). Seldom in the history of writing has an author departed so egregiously from his stated intention. In the autobiography, Bryan dwells exclusively upon himself. Virtually every page is studded with I's. Rarely does Bryan step outside himself and adopt the role of observer or analyst; all persons, events, and subjects have importance only as they relate to him. Perhaps the statement of intent itself should have prepared us for this result: anyone announcing an intention to purge his memoirs of egotism is, at the same time, revealing an egotistic impulse to be fought against and the lack of literary control that might make this struggle successful.

We reach the conclusion that Bryan's posture of self-effacement in the preface is contrived; it is an effort to achieve the appearance of something the man is not. In the preface alone, we can see that Bryan is preoccupied with status. Many of the status themes, which appear consistently throughout the book, are already apparent: ambition, glory, the respect of others, defensiveness and sensitivity to criticism, and the stress on self-importance. The attempt to hide these preoccupations by giving the appearance of self-effacement simply constitutes another status indication.

Bryan continues to focus on success throughout the book. On page 16, Bryan's father is quoted as saying of his son, "He will be President some day," while on the following page, Bryan tells us about his own ambitions before the age of six. On page 60, we are told that the best forum for the orator is the debate, "because it is the form of public speaking that wins the largest victories and gives the greatest renown." He cannot resist mentioning that he was appointed to the House Ways and Means Committee "during my first term when I was only a little past thirty" (p. 158), or that in the 1912 Nebraska primary "I ran about five thousand ahead of the ticket..." (p. 160). Finally, returning to his earlier theme in the preface, Bryan reminds us that "millions of people," the "virtuous masses," toil ceaselessly in anonymity while "those whom they so faithfully support receive the glory" (p. 203).

This stress on fame and recognition dictates the organization of Bryan's work. Most of the autobiography can be placed in two general categories. The first category consists of five chapters concerning Bryan's political career, his strategies and maneuverings:

V. Early National Conventions (4 pages)
VI. A Brief History of the Chicago Convention (18 pages)
VII. Leading Up to My Second Nomination (10 pages)
IX. The St. Louis Convention (14 pages)
X. The Baltimore Convention (29 pages)

A sampling of material, picked from three of these five chapters, shows Bryan's personal political focus. Here, for instance, is how he describes the 1892 Convention:

> The Democratic National Convention of 1892 was held at Chicago. I was a member of Congress then and was renominated a few days before the convention, in fact, went from the Congressional Convention to the Chicago Convention. By this time I had become acquainted with a good many public men and also with a good many politicians. I spoke at Creston in the Boies Campaign the fall of 1891. Here I met a prominent Democratic politician of

that section by the name of Duggan. I happened to meet him at Chicago and learned from him that he was doorkeeper. He offered to let any of my friends in and I soon found out how easily one could add to his list of friends when he could reward them with admission to the national convention. Before the sessions were over I had put a liberal number of western Democrats under obligation to me by bringing them into acquaintance with Mr. Duggan.

At the Chicago Convention I heard Bourke Cockran make his celebrated speech against the third nomination of Mr. Cleveland, but took no part in the convention's deliberations. (P. 99)

The above represents Bryan's every word on the 1892 convention. The focus is exclusively on himself. His acquaintanceship with the "prominent" doorkeeper is apparently more important to him than telling us who won the nomination, how, and why.

This same focus on self characterizes Bryan's description of subsequent conventions. Here, for instance, is a passage on the 1904 Convention, which rejected Bryan for Alton B. Parker:

After being up all night for two nights—one night on the Committee on Resolutions and another at the convention (and I had only slept for a few hours for several preceding nights)—I was utterly exhausted and as soon as I concluded my speech, I returned to the hotel and retired. In fact, it was more than fatigue. I went to the convention with a severe cold and it developed so far as to threaten pneumonia. It was against the advice of my physician that I attended the convention, and the first night I attended the meeting of the Committee on Resolutions wearing a mustard plaster over my chest. As soon as I reached the hotel the doctor put a plaster of antiphlogistine on my chest and I remained in bed until night. During the day Judge Parker sent his famous telegram which threw the convention into an uproar. The delegates brought me news from time to time and no one could foresee the result. Several delegates came over and expressed themselves in very emphatic language to the effect that they "had been bunkoed." I tried to soothe them by telling them that it was no more than they might have expected and that they ought to have known from the tactics

pursued that it was not a compromise which had been demanded but a surrender.
Finally the situation became so tense that I decided to go over to the convention. Taking advantage of the absence of the physician, I dressed and hurried over, pale and worn. I went to the platform and made my last stand against the Parker element. (Pp. 154-55)

In discussing the convention, Bryan never relaxes the focus on himself. His perspective borders on solipsism: nothing happens unless it happens to him. His heroic struggle against a chest cold looms larger than what happened at the convention hall when he was away.

Bryan's egocentricity is sharply revealed in the chapter on the 1912 Democratic Convention, which nominated Woodrow Wilson. Most of it is devoted to Bryan's maneuverings, his speeches, his personal triumphs, and his occasional setbacks. Only in one sentence just before the last paragraph of this twenty-nine-page chapter do we learn that the convention finally chose Wilson. The following passage is typical:

As soon as it was evident that I was defeated [for the post of temporary chairman] I went with my wife and children to the hotel. They were naturally disappointed and sympathetic, but I explained to them why I had made the fight and assured them that my purpose had been accomplished. I was satisfied that the country would be aroused when it knew that a supposedly progressive convention had selected as temporary chairman the man most conspicuously identified with the Wall Street side.

I was not disappointed. I had scarcely reached the hotel before telegrams of congratulations began to pour in. Then followed such a demonstration of the power of public opinion as has never been witnessed in a convention before or since....

....Telegrams continued to pour in.... I received 1182 telegrams and they averaged three names to a telegram. One of them, from Virginia, was signed by one hundred and forty names. (Pp. 169-70)

Here Bryan manages to make his defeat for a particular office sound like a glorious popular victory. He lovingly dwells on the specific details of his "triumph": exactly 1,182 telegrams (did he count each one?), three names to a telegram, one signed by 140 people.

In these chapters, then, Bryan dwells upon personal political history. There is little in these chapters that could be classified as objective description. There is no overall perspective such as would be adopted by a writer with an interest in the events themselves. The camera follows only Bryan and his doings; all other events, issues, and personalities recede into a barely noticeable background.

As we noted in the preceding section on David Clark, personally focused discussion of strategy, tactics, and experiences involving career advancement is an important indication of a status incentive. The seventy-five pages Bryan devotes to this topic (38 percent of the two hundred pages in the autobiography) make it the most prominent subject in the book. Hence, we are led to infer a status incentive for Bryan.

The second general category of material in the autobiography consists of three chapters in which Bryan defends himself against criticism:

    III. At the Bar (24 pages)
  VIII. The Bennett Will Case (16 pages)
    XI. The Grape Juice Incident (3 pages)

The opening paragraph of "At the Bar" explains the nature and purpose of the chapter:

> Political opponents have sometimes referred to me as an unsuccessful lawyer; one president of a great eastern university in a campaign speech delivered in my home city in 1896 argued that I was unfit for the Presidency because I had never enjoyed a large income from my profession. I will not attempt to urge in my behalf

the argument that turned Disraeli from the law to politics, that is: "To succeed as an advocate, I must be a great lawyer, and to be a great lawyer, I must give up my chance of being a great man"; but I think I owe it to my friends to give them a glimpse of my career as a lawyer. From this they can form an estimate as to whether I would have succeeded had I continued in the profession. (P. 61)

In this chapter Bryan minutely recounts his legal career to show that he would surely have been a successful lawyer had he not directed his energy into politics.

In the chapter on the Bennett will, Bryan defends himself against the "malicious misrepresentation" that he had attempted to defraud a widow out of her legacy. He recounts all the particulars of the case in an effort to vindicate himself.

In "The Grape Juice Incident," Bryan defends himself against critics opposing his policy of serving nonalcoholic beverages at formal political dinners. At numerous other points in the work, Bryan shows sensitivity toward those who disagree with him. He refers to "unfair criticism" of him by friends of Congressman Champ Clark (p. 161), to a hostile editorial in the *St. Louis Post Dispatch* (p. 148), to "unfriendly papers" who criticized him for entering the army in 1898 (p. 120), and so forth. The very last words of his autobiography are, "a multitude of cruel and unjust criticisms" (which Bryan says can be dispelled by one act of devotion by one friend).

The substantial space devoted to self-defense indicates that Bryan was easily wounded by criticism, and, by inference, highly anxious to be respected, to be thought well of. All politicians are not so thin skinned. Certain other incentive types — such as the obligation, program, and game types — take criticism pretty much in stride. When, therefore, we encounter a politician who is particularly defensive, the inference we draw is that he is unusually anxious about his public reputation; that is, he appears to have a status incentive.

Two other chapters in the autobiography are especially noteworthy. One, entitled "The Lure of the College Prize" (twelve pages), begins as follows:

> I felt the lure of prizes from the start and took part in every contest for which I was eligible. A prize always stirred me to activity, and a recollection of its influence upon my studies has led me in later days to stimulate students to similar activity by the establishing of prizes in a number of institutions of learning. (P. 85)

With these words Bryan unwittingly reports a status orientation. Prizes and awards, after all, are pure forms of recognition and esteem accorded by others. Bryan's self-proclaimed obsession with prizes thus reveals him to be preoccupied with external approval. Significantly, in this entire chapter Bryan reports virtually nothing about the substance of the debate, oration, and essay contests in which he took part; instead, he focuses upon the prize and his preoccupation with winning it. The following is a typical excerpt:

> In the freshman year I entered the declamation contest for the third time, after having divided the second prize in Latin prose composition with a fellow student. I was gaining ground. In my first contest I came down toward the last, in my second contest I ranked third, in my third contest I won half of the second prize, in my fourth contest—freshman declamation—I rose a point higher and had the second prize all to myself. I did not like dramatic pieces, but at the earnest solicitation of my instructor in rhetoric I took Bernardo del Carpio for my freshman declamation. Of course, the matter was very much on my mind during the days immediately preceding the contest, so much so that a night or two before the declaimers were to appear in public on the stage of Strawn's Opera House I had a dream that made an indelible impression upon me because it came true. In my dream, we seemed to have finished our declamations and were waiting the announcement of the award of the prizes—a moment of great suspense, as all will admit who have passed through the experience. Then the

chairman of the committee of judges appeared and wrote upon the blackboard the names of the victors. I could see my name very distinctly occupying the second place, but I could not make out the name of the man who was awarded the first prize.

My dream not only assured me of my success in securing second prize but it even disclosed to me the books which I selected (the prizes were given in books to be selected by the students themselves. The second prize in this case was $10.00). I selected an Oxford Bible with a concordance and a volume of Shakespeare. As I am writing these words I turn to this treasure and find on the first page of the Bible the following: at the top the Greek letters Sigma Pi and my class '81 and following that these words: "Presented to W. J. Bryan, Salem, Illinois, by the faculty of Illinois College, May 28, 1878. Second prize in declamation." The copy of Shakespeare bound in calf is still in my library and on the first page is a duplicate of the first page of the Bible above referred to. (Pp. 86–87)

Over forty years later, Bryan can recount in detail this dream he had about winning a prize for oratory. Yet he never tells us what he said in any of his prize-winning speeches on such momentous issues as "Justice," "Labor," and "Pauperism, Its Causes and Remedies." His focus is on the external reward, never on the intrinsic subject matter of the speech.

One other chapter of particular interest, the last chapter, is entitled "Friendships" (eleven pages). It strikingly reveals Bryan's preoccupation with personal loyalty. It begins as follows:

So much is flippantly told about the fair-weather friends in politics who flock about the successful candidate and then desert him in times of trial, that I shall take this opportunity to record a few instances of heroes who came under my personal observation. (P. 198)

Bryan then describes eleven individuals and the manner in which they remained his supporters in spite of pressures to the contrary. The chapter appears to be mistitled. It mentions several individuals who were but passing acquaintances, and therefore not "friends" in the usual sense. But in discussing some obviously long-standing friends, Bryan dwells only upon their loyalty to him. The reader is left wondering whether any other characteristics of these people—their humor, their intellect, their interests (beyond Bryan)—were valued by Bryan.

What is the source of this preoccupation with loyalty? Consider the implications of "disloyalty." Assume a supporter becomes an opponent: someone who had praised you now repudiates you. A politician preoccupied with his public reputation is more likely than others to interpret such changes in support personally, as reflecting a loss of the personal esteem of the supporter, and he will be wounded by this loss.

A preoccupation with personal loyalty, then, reflects a preoccupation with status. We have encountered this concern with loyalty in a number of status types we have interviewed; the appearance of this theme in the autobiography further supports the conclusion that Bryan had a status incentive.

Perhaps the most significant feature of the Bryan autobiography is what it does not contain. *It does not contain a single significant reference to policy issues.* Nowhere does Bryan analyze public policy questions. Nowhere does he explore the benefits and disadvantages of various measures. In fact, for most of the dozens of issues on which Bryan took a clear public stand, it is impossible to infer from his autobiography even what his position was!

This omission is most revealing on the issue presumably closest to Bryan's heart, the one that propelled him to national attention: free silver. In the eighteen-page chapter on the events leading to his 1896 nomination, Bryan devotes at most five sentences to discussing the policy aspects of this question (p. 113). Nowhere else in the book does he examine the issue. We never learn why Bryan is for bimetallism, what facts could be marshalled in its favor, or what he thinks its effects on the country might be. The chapter presents in detail Bryan's strategy for winning the nomination and his maneuvers at the convention. He tells exactly when and for how long he spoke during his famous "cross of gold" speech, how the audience reacted to the speech, what people said to him about it later, and so forth. He never tells us, however, what he said in the speech. The issue of bimetallism is not even secondary. It does not matter at all.

For those schooled in the public image of Bryan, the omission of policy discussion is quite startling. Indeed, it is so incongruous that some scholars simply ignore this aspect of the autobiography and trust instead the public image. One biographer, for example, asserts that, compared with other politicians, "Bryan was different. He was an ideologist devoted to a body of serious political beliefs that were germane to society's central problems, and he was willing to place them above victory."[2]

But how devoted could he have been if, when given two hundred pages to express what was on his mind, he neglected even to discuss these beliefs? In those two hundred pages, Bryan is interested enough in the exact hour of his birth to spend half a page on the subject; he spends a full page on the mispronunciation of his name; he recollects in vivid detail his childhood anxieties about winning school prizes. Yet when it comes to this "body of serious political beliefs" he was purportedly "devoted to," Bryan could not spare a paragraph. The conclusion seems inescapable: Bryan did not care very much about the substance of the policies he advocated.

It is true that Bryan did not finish his autobiography; his wife reports that the work represents a first draft. Perhaps he planned to expand the book to cover policy matters? Even if true, this speculation leaves our conclusion unaltered. An author would write first on those subjects of greatest interest to him; to leave policy matters to a revision already testifies to their secondary importance. Furthermore, the autobiography is chronologically complete. Bryan covers the conventions and campaigns in which we know he voiced his issue positions. They would naturally arise in his discussion of these events had he been sufficiently preoccupied with them.

Even in the few references he does make to policies in the autobiography, Bryan reveals their secondary position in his thinking. One illustration appears in "The Grape Juice Incident." The issue was, briefly, Bryan's refusal, as secretary of state, to serve alcoholic beverages at a formal dinner. The incident became known and gave rise to critical commentary in the press. Bryan concludes his reply to critics:

> Within two years the war had aroused so much interest in the liquor question in foreign nations that a number of the crowned heads of Europe were lining up against intoxicating drinks. Then I received my reward. The papers began to cartoon me as driving a water wagon with kings crowding each other for a seat on the vehicle. (P. 189)

Notice how Bryan defines his "reward." One whose primary preoccupation was the policy of abstinence might have put it: "Then I received my reward. The crowned heads of Europe lined up against intoxicating drinks." For Bryan, however, the abstinence of kings (the policy) was secondary; the "reward" was favorable newspaper publicity.

A more complete picture of how issues fit into Bryan's thinking is given in a letter he wrote to Champ Clark, a candidate for the Democratic presidential nomination in 1912. Bryan was at this time supporting Clark (though he later switched to Woodrow Wilson).

> Ft. Wayne, Ind.
> May 30
>
> My dear Clark: —
>
> I venture to make a suggestion for your consideration. I believe the fight over wool will prove a crisis in your life as well as in the

party's prospects. A leader must *lead;* it is not always pleasant to oppose friends, and one who leads takes the chances of defeat, but these are the necessary attendants upon leadership. Wilson is making friends because he *fights.* His fight against Smith was heroic. He fought for the income tax and for a primary law. The people like a fighter. You won your position by fighting and you must continue to fight to hold it. Enter into the wool fight. Don't be content to take polls and sit in the background. Take one side or the other and take it *strong.* If a tax on wool is right, lead the protectionists to victory. You can do it and it will make you strong with that wing of the party. If free wool is right, as I believe it is, lead the fight for it and get the credit for the victory if victory comes. Don't inquire about how the fight is going to go—make it go the right way if you can. If you fail you lay the foundation for a future victory. The right wins in the end—don't be afraid to wait. My opinion is that you will not have to wait long, but whether long or not, one can better afford to be defeated fighting for the right than to win on the wrong side. I hope you will pardon this intrusion upon your thoughts, but the party needs your assistance—a blast from your bugle may save the day, and it will, in my judgment, strengthen you personally.

Regards to the family.

Yours,

Bryan

(P. 163)

At first glance, Bryan appears to be taking an obligation stance, voicing the view that "it's better to be right than to win." Closer inspection reveals, however, that "doing the right thing" has become entangled with expediency in a way an obligation participant would never allow. Bryan recommends taking a position and fighting for it as strategies for personal success because "the people like a fighter." Taking a position pays off because you either "get credit" for victory, or "lay the foundation for future victory." This tactic is recommended to Clark as a posture that will "strengthen you personally."

Notice how flippantly Bryan treats the wool issue. In a brief aside, he notes that he opposes the tariff, but he does not pause to give his reasons or urge Clark to the same point of view. The substance of the wool issue does not interest Bryan, either as a question of wise policy (the program perspective) or as a moral issue (the obligation perspective). Instead, Bryan focuses upon the appearance that taking a stand, any stand, will create. For Bryan, position taking is not something compelled by one's commitment to policy questions; it is a strategy that leads to political success. This perspective closely parallels David Clark's view of "sincerity" as instrumental for personal success.

We return, then, to a point raised early in our discussion of Bryan as an "idealist": he was a vocal, voluble position taker. He also had a status incentive. This paradoxical combination of "idealistic" behavior and status motivation is not at all rare. Status participants want attention and respect. What better way to gain these than to appear as forthright leaders of popular causes? As Bryan put it, the appearance of strong leadership on an issue will "strengthen you personally." It pays off in that strongest of political currencies: name recognition.

This position-taking strategy can pay off in another way. Curiously enough, status participants may be the ones who gain the image of being "hard-working, issue-oriented" leaders. Since they are always taking stands on public questions, they would appear, on the surface, to the press and to the general public, as hard workers with programmatic concerns.

For reasons we shall explain later, program participants are less likely than status participants to get publicity or to take vocal public stands. Hence, they do not create an image of themselves as zealous policy formulators. Paradoxically, then, those public figures who gain recognition as diligent issue activists may turn out to be status participants, for whom the actual working out of public policy is secondary to their preoccupation with public recognition.[3]

Should politicians like Bryan, who are preoccupied with public recognition and lack a deep interest in policy, be called "opportunists"? Once again we must be wary of popular terminology. The term "opportunist" embodies the same type of fallacy inherent in the term "idealist": it lumps a number of qualities together in a stereotype that, empirically, rarely occurs.

One aspect of the term "opportunist" refers to egocentric motivation. On this level, the term would appear to fit Bryan. But another facet of the term refers to the sincerity with which beliefs are held. An opportunist is thought to be one who adopts a position, for reasons of political expedience, although he privately disagrees with the position he has been compelled to take.

Our research on politicians reveals that opportunism in this sense is exceedingly rare among all incentive types, including the status type. To "live a lie" is psychologically taxing; few people — and few politicians — are able to do so to any extensive degree. We have not found cases of politicians who privately repudiate — or even doubt — their publicly taken positions.[4]

We see no reason to believe that Bryan held personal views at variance with his public stands. To the contrary, we are fairly convinced that he was sincere. He actually believed his positions were wise and necessary for the country; if elected, he would have worked toward the implementation of these measures.

We do not find, then, that the status incentive produces insincere or hypocritical policy stands. The status participant may be somewhat superficial in adopting policy positions, and he may not ponder deeply the implications of his proposals. But he normally believes in their rightness.

3 The Program Incentive

THE POLITICIAN WITH A program incentive gets his satisfaction from working on public policy. He enjoys collecting pertinent information, analyzing consequences, drafting measures, and bringing about desired changes.

At first, the program participant seems to be a familiar type. After all, the business of government is policy; therefore, one might reason, most politicians must be "policy-oriented" types. Furthermore, when we see politicians, they are nearly always talking about policy, often stridently enough to be designated "idealists" or "ideologists." Politicians seeking policies seem to abound everywhere; therefore, the reader might easily conclude that he already knows the program-type participant well.

Unfortunately, this supposition would be inaccurate. Program participants are quite different from the popular images of "idealistic," "ideological," or "policy-oriented" politicians. In describing the program incentive, therefore, it is important that we first correct the likely misunderstandings about this type of participant.

1. The program incentive (like all other incentives) is a psychological need. It is not any particular policy goal. The usual image of a policy-oriented politician's "motive" is a particular policy objective: a law, a highway, a housing program. The program incentive should not be equated with having policy goals. Virtually all politicians have such goals. What distinguishes the program type is that he desires to work on specific policy issues and gets positive satisfaction from his work.

2. Because the program participant works on policy matters for his own pleasure, his incentive, or drive, is just as "selfish" as any other incentive. This conception differs from the usual image of policy-oriented leaders as "altruistic"—that is, consciously sacrificing themselves for the benefit of others. The program participant engages in problem solving not because he "ought to," but because he likes to. Hence, terms like "duty," "obligation," or "self-sacrifice" do not describe him appropriately. These terms could more readily apply to obligation or mission participants, whose satisfaction does not come from working on policy matters.

3. The program participant is neither a militant nor a crowd pleaser. Here again, the popular image of a determined, policy-concerned idealist does not fit the program incentive. Usually, we judge public men from a distance. In doing so, we often use the "sound and fury" method for inferring policy commitments. That is, we assume that those politicians who take the most forceful and dramatic public policy stands are in fact the most committed to problem solving and policy achievement. Our image of this type carries strong overtones of militancy and intransigence. We often speak of these men as "idealistic fighters for the public good." (Bryan, for instance, was often described in these terms.)

There is a relationship between militancy and the program incentive, but it is precisely the opposite of the popular image! Program participants are noticeably moderate, restrained, and objective in their attitudes. For reasons we shall explain below, these qualities appear regularly in participants with a program incentive. Hence, when from afar we see an "uncompromising idealist," we can be almost certain that he does not have a program incentive—that is, he is not a politician who gets his satisfaction from devising and implementing policy. The "uncompromising idealist" image is, in fact, consistent with several incentives other than program: for example, status (William Jennings Bryan), obligation, even adulation or mission.

The program incentive, then, is the satisfaction that flows from working upon governmental policies. It is (1) not defined as merely having specific policy goals, (2) a genuine satisfaction and, therefore, not properly thought of as a self-sacrificing motive, and (3) neither defined by, nor associated with, vigorous public position-taking.

In interviews, the program incentive is recognized, first, by the interest a respondent exhibits in substantive policy issues. There are, to be sure, other traits of the program type, but this focus on substantive issues is the primary one. The program participant gets his satisfaction from working on policy questions; it is, therefore, natural that in an unstructured, informal interview he will gravitate toward discussing policy.

As it happens, all politicians — regardless of incentive — work a good deal on policy matters. The nature of the job forces all of them to become familiar with, or even expert on, policy questions. Furthermore, politicians are expected to display interest and competence in policy matters. For these reasons, much policy discussion occurs more or less inevitably in any interview with any politician and cannot serve to identify his incentive. Policy discussion may arise from a politician's wish to answer questions responsively, to impress, or to make conversation. Such policy discussion may be called "incidental": it reveals little about the respondent's level of interest in policy. Incidental policy discussion differs significantly from the policy discussion of the program participant, which does reflect a genuine interest in the substance of policy. The main points of difference include the following:

1. The program respondent spontaneously raises or drifts into policy discussion. Others talk on policy matters only when the interview questions or context dictates. The question the

incentive analyst is seeking to answer is not: Can the respondent talk about policy? Almost anyone can. The question is: Does he prefer to talk about policy?

2. The program respondent's discussion of policy is longer on a given topic than an incidental comment. Length alone gives some indication of a respondent's interest.

3. The program respondent focuses upon "small" policy questions; he does not remain at the "broad issue" level. Policy questions are typically treated by the mass media in highly abstract terms: "reordering priorities," "tax reform," "energy crisis." A politician interested in the substance of policy is impelled to go beyond this symbolic level. He wants to be concrete. He wants to examine the specific consequences of specific changes. Starting with "highway safety," for example, he ends up looking into the placement of stop signs. Or the term "energy crisis" is supplanted by an exploration of the technology and costs of reclaiming used engine oil. While others remain at the level of abstraction, he talks about kilowatt hours, tons of gravel, or costs per pupil. Concern about the substance of a policy is a concern about what specific individuals do and how specific policy changes affect their behavior.

4. The program respondent is an empiricist. Interested in substantive policy, he wants to find out what works and what doesn't. He wants his remedies not to be worse than the disease. As a result, his orientation toward policy questions is open, objective, and pragmatic. Of course he has opinions, but he expresses them as judgments based on empirical arguments.

This nondogmatic style contrasts with the manner in which certain other types of politicians express their views. Obligation types, for example, are generally rigid and dogmatic, treating policy questions as black-white moral issues. Many status types also display a dogmatic moralistic style, partly because this approach enhances visibility and projects an appealing image.

5. The program respondent exhibits originality and insight. He brings out little-known facts and relationships. He ignores,

or explicitly contradicts, prevailing clichés and conceptions. The politician who takes a deep personal interest in policy questions will have developed fresh, even iconoclastic, views.

It should be clear from the foregoing that virtually all "policy discussion" we are popularly exposed to in speeches and in the media falls into the "incidental" category. In the typical television interview, for example, the respondent is being forced to make short replies to broad, symbolic-level policy questions. Only at his peril may he contradict the prevailing public perspective, or question a cliché, or go into concrete, boring detail. The interviewer is often out to trap the respondent into an embarrassing headline; the respondent's strategy is to keep the discussion amorphous and unspecific—while, at the same time, projecting an image of competence and concern. Such interviews in the media, then, should not form the basis of any conclusion about incentives.

In the following pages, we shall give some examples of policy discussion by politicians who are genuinely interested in the substantive issues. In this way, the reader will be able to see what this type of material really looks like.

I. WILLIAM HAMMERSMITH: "IN MORRIS COUNTY... YOU CAN BUY CIGARETTES FOR $2.76 A CARTON"

William Hammersmith is beginning his second four-year term as councilman of Creston, a large city in central Virginia.*
He is forty-five years old, an attorney specializing in trial cases.

After preliminary introductions, the interviewer begins with a standard general question about local problems. At first, Hammersmith's answer is nothing more than the standard, incidental policy discussion anyone would give. It looks like this:

---

*The councilman's name and city have been changed.

54 THE PROGRAM INCENTIVE

Q: What are the most important problems you have here?
HAMMERSMITH: Well, 'course there's one great big fat one that we can hit first thing, and that is stretching the dollar in local government to do the work that twenty should be doing. In other words, a budget problem. (slight pause) Well, providing the services that our people are interested in and accustomed to with this present inflationary situation that we've got, and the cost, wage-price increase that we've got, and at the same time, not raising taxes so as to boost the wage-price situation up further. Because that's the one biggest problem, and I find, frankly—and I think the other councilmen would agree—that about three-fourths of our time is involved one way or the other in this same old money squeeze.

This type of material continues for several minutes—an introductory, general description of policy problems. But then, ten minutes into the interview, the conversation takes a distinctive turn. In the typical interview, the policy discussion would have petered out by now, and a new subject of conversation would have taken over. But not in this case. Instead, the policy discussion becomes concrete.

HAMMERSMITH: We've got to have other sources of revenue and right now they're just not available to us. We raised the cigarette tax, the local cigarette tax, just at the last council meeting, because otherwise our budget would have been a deficit budget for this coming year. We raised the cigarette tax two cents a pack, and we raised the utilities taxes, the local utilities tax...
Q: (interrupting) What's that, water?
HAMMERSMITH: Electric power, water, and gas and telephone.
Q: Oh, I see.
HAMMERSMITH: We raised the local tax on that 1 percent. From 9 to 10 percent of the bill. Now, of course, that's passed on to the customer. In fact, the billing method used here is, they show your bill and then they show local tax, so much. So you're not taxing the utilities, you're taxing just about everyone, because telephone, light, and water are no longer luxuries, they're necessities. The cigarette thing, I'm afraid—two reasons I opposed it on council

myself—it was a 4-3 vote, incidentally, for raising both of these. Two reasons that I opposed it, I felt that there were other savings that could have been made. In other words, I felt that the budget could have been more of a responsible budget, really. And secondly, I'm afraid that this raise in cigarette taxes is just going to be a cause of less revenue. Because I think, frankly, that people are going to buy their cigarettes across the river or in the county. Right now you can, as I mentioned in council meeting, you can go right over here on top of the hill in Morris County, not a half a mile from here, and you can buy cigarettes for $2.76 a carton. Right down here on Main Street now the merchants are having to sell them for about $3.50 or something like that, a carton, and a raise of two more cents is going to boost them on up, getting in the neighborhood of $4. So, most people who smoke, particularly who smoke heavily, are going to buy their cigarettes by the carton in the county. I think that any increase in income there is not only going to be problematical, but I think it's just not going to materialize. I think we may lose money by that.

Hammersmith has left the generalities with which the interview began, and has focused on a small policy issue, which he illustrates with a specific examination of individual psychology and behavior. And he does not stop here. Aided only by minimal interviewer probes (which say, in effect, "I'm interested if you still are"), Hammersmith doggedly explores all aspects of the fiscal situation for twenty more minutes. A sample of the continuation looks like this:

HAMMERSMITH: Of course, we could raise real estate taxes. But right now, most of us feel that real estate is bearing its disproportion... a greater proportion of the burden. Our tax rate on real estate now is $3 a hundred. Out in many of the counties, real estate is assessed for tax purposes at anywhere from one-third to one-fifth or one-sixth of value. If you have a $10,000 house, they assess it at anywhere from, say, about $1,500 or $2,000 on up to about... the highest county assessment I know of is about thirty-three and one-third. So you'd have anywhere from about $1,500 up to $3,300 that that $10,000 house would be assessed at. Then their tax rate is applied to that. Some counties have lower, some higher than our $3, but the point is, the assessment itself is so much lower than in the city. Here we assess it at 50 percent of value and then tax it at $3. So, in other words, on a $10,000 house—fair market value $10,000 —you're assessed at $5,000, you pay $3 tax on it: $150 a year, you see. And we feel like the real estate is already bearing its cost.

Notice the empirical, concrete, nondogmatic focus of this treatment. Hammersmith is not painting grand pictures; he is not moralizing; he is not criticizing. He is chugging through a methodical analysis of the concrete policy problem.

Scarcely has the fiscal policy analysis been concluded when policy arises again, in the following manner:

> Q: You said you enjoyed it. What aspect or...
> HAMMERSMITH: I enjoy...as the only lawyer on city council here...and one thing that I had in mind when I agreed to run was I felt like, and most of the lawyers felt like, there was a great deal that needed to be done in improving our courts, and our system of bail, our system of warrants, the workings of our lower courts, our minicipal court, our police court, our civil court, our juvenile court. And we have reorganized those since I've been on council. We have reorganized those a great deal. We have combined a couple of courts' clerks' offices, at a great deal of saving. We completely renovated the system for bailing people and for issuing warrants and that sort of thing. I think we've done a great deal from the standpoint of giving our people better court and legal services.

Of course, it fits the description of the program type that he should report policy work as his area of enjoyment. However, we must be careful not to accept such claims without internal corroboration. Many politicians who do not have a program incentive will say that they like working on policy and bringing about needed changes.

The test for whether a respondent actually gets his principal satisfaction from working on policy is not that he says so; this conclusion must be inferred from the emphasis he gives the topic of policy. When the subject of policy accomplishment comes up, the interviewer is obligated to probe, to give the respondent an opportunity to expand on the subject if he is really interested.

In the interview with David Clark, the status type we met in the preceding chapter, policy accomplishments were mentioned, the interviewer probed, and Clark's reply was brief and superficial. The conclusion was that Clark, whatever he may have claimed, was not primarily preoccupied with working on policy.

Similarly, Hammersmith has given a general summary of a policy accomplishment. The probe question is asked; the answer contrasts dramatically with Clark's:

Q: How did the bailing system change, exactly?

HAMMERSMITH: All right, I can give you, if you're interested in that, I can give you a couple of real obvious examples. It used to be that if you were arrested in Creston on any charge for which you had to be bailed out, you had to post bail. We had an assistant judge, we had two assistant judges who would appear at the police station at ten in the morning, five in the afternoon, and ten at night. Now that was the only time that you could make bail. If you were arrested at eleven at night, for instance — well, of course, if somebody knew me and called me at home, got me out of bed, I could call the judge and get him, probably, to agree to do it. But most people didn't know about this. They'd have to lay up there in jail. Maybe the most prominent citizen, and all kinds of money and everything, and the ability to post bail, but he had to stay up there in jail until ten the next morning, guilty or innocent, you see, to post his bail. Well, we now have round-the-clock bail service. Because... for the last years I've been chairman of the judiciary committee on council, and we have worked it out now so that we have, any time anybody is arrested, we have an assistant judge or a bail commissioner who can admit them to bail, either present at the police station or on call at city hall or within fifteen minutes' availability. That's the rule.

Also, it used to be, when I started practicing law here and until I went on council, that if somebody stole a hundred dollars from you, to take out a warrant for them, you had to go up and swear out a warrant for the person. The assistant judge had a $2 fee for that warrant being sworn out. Now you had to pay $2. Somebody's stolen your $100. You had to pay the judge's $2 fee for him to issue the warrant. So you had to throw your $2 after the $100 you'd already lost. For some reason, one of our previous judges had not wanted his clerks to fool with keeping court costs. So he didn't add court costs to his fines. He'd fine somebody something, but that was it. There was no court cost. Now this is grossly unfair. So we changed the whole concept around.

There is no fee basis now. If you swear a warrant up, the city pays that $2, that is chargeable...it goes into the judge's salary, because that's the only way that we can provide a judge remuneration. But the city pays that, rather than the complainant who's sworn out the warrant. It's added on if the man is fined, say $50 in police court. He's fined $50 and the court costs $6 or $7, whatever it is, which includes that $2 and goes back to the city. If he's found innocent, of course, the city foots the bill on that. But actually, it's worked out, to the amazement of some of my friends — I told them it would all along, but they wouldn't listen. It worked out the first year. We saved about $18,000 for the city in handling it that way, and gave our people a service that they'd never had before.

So many of these things, I feel, like having a lawyer on the council for the first time in years, frankly, have improved our judicial system a great deal. We used to have one judge whose office was up here in this building on the eighth floor, who was our civil judge, who tried civil cases on the lower court basis in our Creston municipal civil court. And he held court three mornings a week at ten. We had another judge who tried all criminal cases at nine every morning. Now, this required two judges, two courtrooms. Neither court was being used except, well, the police court would last from nine till on the average about twelve. Sometimes till two or three, but sometimes it would get out by ten. Never, hardly more than just the morning, for the police court, the criminal court. Now, the civil court, then, would meet in another courtroom: another judge — paying another judge's salary — would meet three mornings a week, Monday, Wednesday, and Friday at ten, and he was never there, or hardly ever there, past twelve. So, what we did, we simply combined the police court and the civil justice court under the same judge and one clerk's office. We moved our clerk from the civil court judge's office into the same clerk's office with the two clerks from the criminal court. It's a much busier court. Put the three women in the same office and made each of them clerks and had each of them learn the other's job so that in sickness or vacations they could each switch around in the job. Only one judge instead of two. He now holds criminal court at nine in the morning and civil court at two in the afternoon, every afternoon and every day during the week. Our people get two more days of civil court than they were getting. We only use one courtroom, the other courtroom could be taken over for other purposes within the city. And there's a tremendous saving and much, much better service right there.

Not a single additional probe by the interviewer has been necessary to elicit this sustained, concrete discussion of a small policy issue. Hammersmith's enthusiasm for the subject is unmistakable. Naturally, he is talking about a policy that he was centrally involved in, and he takes obvious pride in his accomplishments. But the account is not egocentric. The stress is upon the external situation, the workings of the court system. When talking about policy, the program participant says, in effect, "I was involved with a policy issue and now let me tell you about the facts and relationships of that situation." The status type places the emphasis on himself, as if to say, "I was involved with a policy issue and now let me tell you what I did in connection with it."

Substantive policy discussion of the type excerpted above constitutes about 60 percent of the Hammersmith interview. The second most salient topic, about 15 percent of the interview, is policy-making procedure. It is natural that a politician interested in the substance of policy would also be interested in the process of making policy; this interest is another characteristic of the program type.

One illustration of Hammersmith's interest in policy-making procedure concerns holding executive sessions:

Q: Do you think that all council meetings should be made public?

HAMMERSMITH: No. Not all of them. No. There are some matters that would be utterly stupid to consider in public. For instance, acquisition of property for a fire station. If we brought that up in public that we were interested in getting a fire station location in, say, the such-and-such hundred block of Ripmont Avenue, well, my Lord, we'd pay six times for the property what we would pay if we met in secret — as the paper says, a "secret" session, an executive session — and decided on it and sent out somebody in our real estate department up here to obtain an option and then made it public.

In other words, we discuss these matters in private or executive session, but any action that is taken, any valid vote that is taken, has to be taken in public session. But we discuss these matters in private, and pretty well get either an option or a contract or what have you, to tie up the property before we announce we're interested in it. Otherwise, we'd just balloon the price on everything, and the poor old taxpayer has to pay through the nose for everything.

So, the same is true for personnel. You can't decide...for instance, you can't go up there in an open council session and have seven members of the council, each one of them suggest a different person for membership on the city school board and proceed to thrash out the advantages and disadvantages of some seven leading citizens here in an open session. It's much better to meet and more or less decide who you're going to appoint, and then come out in an open session and vote on it and so forth.

The length of the comment and the concrete illustrations indicate that the subject of secret versus open sessions is one Hammersmith cares about and has thought about. We also notice a certain independent, iconoclastic orientation. Hammersmith ignores the popular media perspective in which "open meetings" is gospel and instead offers an incisive defense of secrecy. He is unconcerned with the image that he might project to a mass audience (headline: HAMMERSMITH URGES SECRECY IN GOVERNMENT). He is interested only in convincing the interviewer.

We see from this illustration how program and status types tend to be evaluated differently, depending upon the distance from which one views them. Status types address and appeal to the inattentive mass audiences lying beyond the immediate personal context. As a result, they are more impressive from afar than up close. Program types behave oppositely. They interact with and attempt to convince their immediate audience while being unmindful of the impression they might leave on distant, inattentive onlookers. Consequently, from afar they often project a weak or negative image.

Another characteristic of the program type is the stress he places on information, on being informed, and on deciding policy questions on their own merits. Naturally, this orientation follows from the program participant's commitment to policy making as the primary task.

A clear illustration of this perspective in the Hammersmith interview occurs in his reply to a question about the quality most important to "succeed." This question is particularly useful because it allows the respondent to supply his own definition of success and thereby reveal the focus of his concern.

Q: What quality or characteristic do you think is most important to be a successful councilman?

HAMMERSMITH: Well, a willingness, I think, to really *try* to be informed about what's going on and keeping up on what's going on, and sort of doing your homework, as it were. This is a part-time job, of necessity that's what it is. You can't give but so much time to it if you're busy, and I suppose everybody on our council here is. I know they are. So you've got to try to get as much information as you can so as to act as intelligently, or from as well-informed a position as you can, yet realizing that you can't get all the information you'd like. You've got to try to get as much information as you can, and keep current on it.

With all the possible answers to choose from—"sincerity," "friends," "integrity," "compassion," "popularity," and so on—Hammersmith confines his reply to the importance of information and making intelligent decisions.

This same focus on policy making is exhibited in Hammersmith's definition of his own role:

Q: Well, to shift the question a little bit, what do you see as the most important aspect of your job as a councilman?
HAMMERSMITH: The *most* important single aspect?
Q: Yah.
HAMMERSMITH: Well, I suppose you would say, being a member of what in effect is a board of directors of a $20 million corporation. I mean a corporation dealing in about $20 million budget a year. That's the main thing, it seems to me.

Again we notice an unusual response. Most politicians, when asked this question, will make some reference to the democratic context. They will say their most important job is "to bring government closer to the people," or "to provide leadership," or "to encourage citizen involvement." Hammersmith ignores this aspect altogether. His choice of analogies is striking. A member of a corporate board of directors is not, practically speaking, popularly elected; he does not do things to make people happy; he does not get publicity; he does not mingle with crowds or friends; he even has a slightly negative image. All he does is make decisions. Apparently that is all Hammersmith is thinking of in describing his role.

Hammersmith's interest in policy and policy making is complemented by an utter lack of interest in the mechanics of position getting. In the previous chapter, we noted that position getting was of central concern to status types. In fact, all other incentive types find some aspect of position getting of interest to them—including obligation types, who get the opportunity to stand up for principle during campaigns. Only program types do not find the history and mechanics of position getting a rewarding topic of conversation. It is natural that this should be so. The position-getting phase of politics is devoid of policy-making satisfactions. As a result, interviews with program types are generally shallow in accounts of the respondent's own campaign and election activities. One almost gets the impression that the subject fell out of the sky into his present position. Here is Hammersmith's entire reply on the subject of personal political history:

Q: I'm interested in the careers and political histories of councilmen. How did you first get interested in politics?

HAMMERSMITH: Well, I've only been in Creston eleven years. I was not born and raised here.

Q: Where?

HAMMERSMITH: Out in southwest Virginia. Galax, Virginia. In fact, I practiced law in Stewart, Virginia, which was the county seat of Patrick County, before I came here. I've only been here eleven years. When I was there in Stewart, I was town attorney, but that was not an elected job. Well, I was elected by the town council, but to represent the city legally.

When I came to Creston...I don't know really how I could pin it down, except just that this is...a situation, where, when it comes time for council election, people—certain groups, certain people—try to prevail upon those people that they think apparently would...would make a good councilman to run for the office. And I did *not* have, either time I had run, the backing of

either of the major parties. I didn't seek it. I ran as an Independent.
Q: Oh really? On the ballot?
HAMMERSMITH: That's right. As an Independent. And...so it was just a matter of my friends and so forth wanting me to run, and I agreed to do it and first thing I knew, I was in the middle of it. But I do have and I suppose most any lawyer, most lawyers, have some interest in government, because our business takes us so much into that — various commissions and courts and so forth. But I never thought of myself as being so very politically inclined. I don't have any further intentions with regards to any state office or anything like that. Had groups coming to see me about the state legislature and so forth from time to time before election. And I tell them, I've got troubles enough now, here just on the local basis without getting into that. (laughs) I must say I do enjoy it, except for... my practice and my time are just such that I don't think that I'll be able to continue after this eight years.

Hammersmith is vague and brief about his election campaigns. He can talk nonstop for ten minutes on judicial reform, yet when it comes to his own struggle to reach office, he does not recall a single tactic or incident. We notice also the hobby-like orientation of the program type in this comment. Hammersmith is drawn to politics by his interest in the subject matter; he enjoys working on the substantive issues. But he does not view politics as an all-consuming passion, as a necessity, or as a crusade. Other activities, particularly his occupation, represent his primary commitment.

In broad terms, a program type like Hammersmith resembles a policymaking machine. Policy is his central preoccupation and virtually his only preoccupation. The cares and concerns of most politicians seem to be left out of his constitution. He is not personally concerned with winning friends, with popularity, with moralistic stands at the gates, or with projecting any kind of image to a distant audience. He does not react to people personally, as if they—or he—had anxieties, frustrations, or insecurities. He treats others almost as a computer would treat them: as sources of policy information, analysis, and opinion. Hammersmith, in fact, appears quite insensitive to others' reaction to him. Notice how casually he shrugs off personal criticism:

> Q: (interrupting) Do you find, as a councilman, that you get a lot of criticism?
> HAMMERSMITH: Oh Lord, yeah. But in my business I'm sort of accustomed to that anyhow. I mean, when you practice trial law, you don't expect to please many people, and only the ones on your side of the case. So that just kind of runs off my back. I'm not thin-skinned, and... but it's like what Harry Truman says, if you were, you couldn't be in any political job this day and time (slight chuckle).
>
> Because I firmly believe most people, this day and time, although I hate to say it, but the vast majority of people... the only reaction they show to government—local, state, or federal—is kind of an anti-thing. In other words, unless it treads on their toes, you don't hear much from them. You don't get much commendation. But the minute you step on somebody's toes, you've got a hell of a lot of (laughs) criticism. And you just have to roll with the punches, as far as that goes.

Hammersmith's bemused indifference to the hostility his political actions might generate contrasts vividly with the sense of hurt, outrage, or rancor other politicians might feel.

The consequence of the program type's inattention to public relations is that he is somewhat disadvantaged in a competitive mass-electoral context. He does not work hard at public image building. He does not exert himself to attract attention. His time and effort do not go into campaigning. While close friends may admire him, distant voters see only a colorless image—if they notice him at all.

In a less competitive context, where local notables or party leaders influence the outcome of elections, the program type gains an advantage. Knowing the possible candidates in greater depth, local leaders are likely to prefer program types and, so to speak, do their campaigning and publicity work for them. For instance, the backing of prominent local leaders was apparently instrumental in Hammersmith's election. In races for more sought-after offices (e.g., statewide or congressional posts), a program type such as Hammersmith would clearly be at a disadvantage compared with politicians adept at publicity building—in particular, the status type.

II. Benjamin Franklin: "The Convenience of Having But One Gutter in Such a Narrow Street"

Benjamin Franklin, in addition to all his other activities, was a prolific writer. Among his literary contributions is a remarkably candid, personally focused autiobiography. This document is not a formal historical account. It was written in four parts on four separate occasions spanning nineteen years. Franklin began it at the age of sixty-five as a letter to his son to pass along anecdotes of his early life. In the latter sections, Franklin recognized a wider audience, but still he maintained the same tone of personal reminiscence. As befits a personally focused autobiography, Franklin wrote it from memory; it exhibits several errors of historical sequence and dating. It is a personally oriented document, then, of the type suitable for incentive analysis.

As we have said, incentive analysis treats only one aspect of a personality, the emotional need underlying political participation. With a figure so versatile as Franklin, this focus causes us to ignore most of what the man was: entrepreneur, inventor, scientist, journalist, philosopher. The discussion that follows, therefore, by no means gives a comprehensive picture of Franklin. It is only the man of public affairs, treated mainly in the third section of the autobiography, that we examine.[1]

Franklin is known for his many contributions to his community: he founded Philadelphia's lending library, fire department, hospital, and so on. Knowledge of these deeds, however, does not form a basis for ascribing an incentive to Franklin. Incentives are determined not by accomplishments (or reputed accomplishments), but by the orientation of the individual. How did Franklin feel about these projects? What was the depth of his preoccupation with the substance of policy? These are the kinds of questions we must answer to determine his incentive.

A comparison with William Jennings Bryan is instructive. Both Bryan and Franklin have gone down in history as figures clearly associated with certain public issues. But the parallel ends there. Bryan, as we saw from an examination of his autobiography, had but a superficial interest in policy matters. On most issues, he neglects even to mention what his position was, and he never gives an analysis of the details, causes, or consequences of any measure.

Franklin is exactly the reverse. Part III of his autobiography dwells extensively on policy matters discussed in exhaustive detail. Unlike Bryan, Franklin is genuinely preoccupied with the substance of policy.

The excerpt that follows is typical of Franklin's discussion of policy issues. Here he is recounting his proposal for improving the condition of the streets of London:

> I had observ'd that the streets, when dry, were never swept, and the light dust carried away; but it was suffer'd to accumulate till wet weather reduc'd it to mud, and then, after lying some days so deep on the pavement that there was no crossing but in paths kept clean by poor people with brooms, it was with great labour rak'd together and thrown up into carts open above, the sides of which suffer'd some of the slush at every jolt on the pavement to shake out and fall, sometimes to the annoyance of foot-passengers. The reason given for not sweeping the dusty street was, that the dust would fly into the windows of shops and houses.
>
> An accidental occurrence had instructed me how much sweeping might be done in a little time. I found at my door in Craven-street, one morning, a poor woman sweeping my pavement with a birch

broom; she appeared very pale and feeble, as just come out of a fit of sickness. I ask'd who employ'd her to sweep there; she said, "Nobody; but I am very poor and in distress, and I sweeps before gentlefolkses doors, and hopes they will give me something." I bid her sweep the whole street clean, and I would give her a shilling; this was at nine o'clock; at twelve she came for the shilling. From the slowness I saw at first in her working, I could scarce believe that the work was done so soon, and sent my servant to examine it, who reported that the whole street was swept perfectly clean, and all the dust plac'd in the gutter, which was in the middle; and the next rain wash'd it quite away, so that the pavement and even the kennel were perfectly clean.

I then judg'd that, if that feeble woman could sweep such a street in three hours, a strong, active man might have done it in half the time. And here let me remark the convenience of having but one gutter in such a narrow street, running down its middle, instead of two, one on each side, near the footway; for where all the rain that falls on a street runs from the sides and meets in the middle, it forms there a current strong enough to wash away all the mud it meets with; but when divided into two channels, it is often too weak to cleanse either, and only makes the mud it finds more fluid, so that the wheels of carriages and feet of horses throw and dash it upon the foot-pavement, which is thereby rendered foul and slippery, and sometimes splash it upon those who are walking. (Pp. 728-29)

Franklin proceeds to detail his proposal for gathering dirt from the streets of London, and then continues with his afterthoughts on such matters as the construction and placement of the carts for collecting the dirt. Then he concludes:

Some may think these trifling matters not worth minding or relating; but when they consider that tho' dust blown into the eyes of a single person, or into a single shop on a windy day, is but of small importance, yet the great number of the instances in a populous city, and its frequent repetitions give it weight and consequence, perhaps they will not censure very severely those who bestow some attention to affairs of this seemingly low nature. Human felicity is produc'd not so much by great pieces of good fortune that seldom happen, as by little advantages that occur every day. Thus, if you teach a poor young man to shave himself, and keep his razor in order, you may contribute more to the happiness of his life than in giving him a thousand guineas. The money may be soon spent, the regret only remaining of having foolishly consumed it; but in the other case, he escapes the frequent vexation of waiting for barbers, and of their sometimes dirty fingers, offensive breaths, and dull razors; he shaves when most convenient to him, and enjoys daily the pleasure of its being done with a good instrument. With these sentiments I have hazarded the few preceding pages, hoping they may afford hints which some time or other may be useful to a city I love, having lived many years in it very happily, and perhaps to some of our towns in America. (P. 730)

This excerpt meets all the criteria for showing a genuine preoccupation with policy. It is spontaneous: at the risk of boring his readers or seeming petty, Franklin digresses on the subject because it interests him. The length of the treatment further reveals his interest. He focuses upon a "small" policy issue: dirt in the streets. An author wishing to appear heroic could hardly choose a less inspiring subject. The discussion is chock full of concrete facts and cause-and-effect observations; Franklin obviously delights in unearthing these points. Finally, the discussion is iconoclastic. Human betterment, says Franklin, is not accomplished by momentous strokes, crusades, or utopian quests, as most of us are disposed to believe. It is accomplished quietly, in small incremental steps.

Again and again we encounter this same type of detailed, concrete policy discussion in the autobiography. For example, Franklin discusses street lighting:

It was by a private person, the late Mr. John Clifton, his giving a sample of the utility of lamps, by placing one at his door, that the people were first impress'd with the idea of enlighting all the city. The honour of this public benefit has also been ascrib'd to me, but it belongs truly to that gentleman. I did but follow his example, and have only some merit to claim respecting the form of our lamps, as differing from the globe lamps we were at first supply'd with from London. Those we found inconvenient in these respects: they admitted no air below; the smoke, therefore, did not readily go out above, but circulated in the globe, lodg'd on its inside, and soon obstructed the light they were intended to afford; giving, besides, the daily trouble of wiping them clean; and an accidental stroke on one of them would demolish it, and render it totally useless. I therefore suggested composing them of four flat panes, with a long funnel above to draw up the smoke, and crevices admitting air below, to facilitate the ascent of the smoke; by this means they were kept clean, and did not grow dark in a few hours, as the London lamps do, but continu'd bright till morning, and an accidental stroke would generally break but a single pane, easily repair'd.

I have sometimes wonder'd that the Londoners did not, from the effect holes in the bottom of the globe lamps us'd at Vauxhall have in keeping them clean, learn to have such holes in their street lamps. But, these holes being made for another purpose, viz., to communicate flame more suddenly to the wick by a little flax hanging down thro' them, the other use, of letting in air, seems not to have been thought of; and therefore, after the lamps have been lit a few hours, the streets of London are very poorly illuminated. (Pp. 727-28)

Elsewhere, Franklin reports on one of his first policy ideas in the following manner:

I began now to turn my thoughts a little to public affairs, beginning, however, with small matters. The city watch was one of the first things that I conceiv'd to want regulation. It was managed by the constables of the respective wards in turn; the constable warned a number of housekeepers to attend him for the night. Those who chose never to attend, paid him six shillings a year to be excus'd, which was suppos'd to be for hiring substitutes, but was, in reality, much more than was necessary for that purpose, and made the constableship a place of profit; and the constable, for a little drink, often got such ragamuffins about him as a watch, that respectable housekeepers did not choose to mix with. Walking the rounds, too, was often neglected, and most of the nights spent in tippling. I thereupon wrote a paper to be read in Junto, representing these irregularities, but insisting more particularly on the inequality of this six-shilling tax of the constables, respecting the circumstances of those who paid it, since a poor widow housekeeper, all whose property to be guarded by the watch did not perhaps exceed the value of fifty pounds, paid as much as the wealthiest merchant, who had thousands of pounds' worth of goods in his stores.

On the whole, I proposed as a more effectual watch, the hiring of proper men to serve constantly in that business; and as a more equitable way of supporting the charge, the levying a tax that should be proportion'd to the property. This idea, being approv'd by the Junto, was communicated to the other clubs, but as arising in each of them; and though the plan was not immediately carried into execution, yet, by preparing the minds of people for the change, it paved the way for the law obtained a few years after, when the members of our clubs were grown into more influence. (Pp. 709-10)

Franklin does not merely give a summary of the issue, as most authors would do; he goes into minute, analytical detail. The vividness of these discussions is all the more remarkable when we consider that Franklin is recalling them many decades later. The proposal on the night watch, for example, was developed when Franklin was about twenty-nine; he was eighty-two when he wrote the report above. After fifty-three years, what Franklin remembers and chooses to recount are the specific details of a policy problem.

Franklin, then, exhibits the principal characteristic of the program incentive type: he is genuinely interested in the substance of policy. Will it work? How does it work? These are the questions that preoccupy him.

In addition to his preoccupation with the substance of policy, Franklin also displays the program type's characteristic interest in the process of policy making. In Franklin's case, this interest is expressed in his accounts of the methods he employed for getting his projects adopted. He repeatedly mentions three points that formed the backbone of his policy-making strategy. First, he would "prepare the minds of the people" by talking up an idea among his friends and by writing in newspapers or pamphlets on the subject. He realized that one cannot successfully surprise the public with a plan; the ground has to be prepared first. Second, Franklin would form a group or association to back the particular idea. He realized that political reform is a collective undertaking; again, he would lay the groundwork by establishing organizational support. Third, Franklin would avoid taking credit for the proposal. Credit claiming, Franklin found, is destructive to carrying out projects; resentments and resistance are stirred up when a promoter insists upon standing at the head of the campaign. Therefore, Franklin made it a rule to "put myself as much as I could out of sight" (p. 623).

These three points are nicely illustrated in Franklin's opening words recounting the founding of the Philadelphia Academy (later to become the University of Pennsylvania):

> Peace being concluded, and the association business therefore at an end, I turn'd my thoughts again to the affair of establishing an academy. The first step I took was to associate in the design a number of active friends, of whom the Junto furnished a good part; the next was to write and publish a pamphlet, entitled *Proposals relating to the Education of Youth in Pennsylvania.* This I distributed among the principal inhabitants gratis; and as soon as I could suppose their minds a little prepared by the perusal of it, I set on foot a subscription for opening and supporting an academy: it was to be paid in quotas yearly for five years; by so dividing it, I judg'd the subscription might be larger, and I believe it was so, amounting to no less, if I remember right, than five thousand pounds.
>
> In the introduction to these proposals, I stated their publication, not as an act of mine, but of some *publick-spirited gentlemen,*

avoiding as much as I could, according to my usual rule, the presenting myself to the publick as the author of any scheme for their benefit. (P. 721)

One should not conclude, incidentally, that Franklin's autobiography is without a trace of vanity. As we shall note later, Franklin does have certain status preoccupations—to which he frankly admits. But his commitment to problem solving outweighs his need for recognition.

Franklin's orientation may be contrasted with that of a status-type politician. For the status type, short-run ego satisfactions are rarely subjugated to the needs of policy making. The status type needs to be recognized as the promoter of a policy. As a result, status types often generate resistance to their proposals. Program types, working persistently but unobtrusively at the substance and organizational details of a policy project, are more likely to be successful.

Another program trait that Franklin exhibits is a concern for maintaining harmonious personal relationships. It is easy to see how this orientation develops. Personal conflicts embitter, confuse, and trammel policy making. A participant who gets his satisfaction from productive policy making comes to see the importance of not letting personal frictions get in the way of the problem-solving process.

Conviviality types, as we shall see, also display a preoccupation with personal harmony. But their orientation is substantially different. The conviviality participant seeks friendship and approval to satisfy his need for social acceptance. He finds hostility personally threatening and companionship personally reassuring. The program type is not greatly affected either by approval or by hostility. For him, harmonious personal relationships are instrumental in obtaining his real satisfaction, productive policy making. Friendship is valued not as a source of reassurance, but as the basis of working relationships with other participants.

Franklin stresses this instrumental aspect of maintaining good personal relationships at many points in the autobiography. In commenting upon Pennsylvania Governor Robert Morris's self-proclaimed "love of disputing," Franklin observes:

> He had some reason for loving to dispute, being eloquent, an acute sophister, and, therefore, generally successful in argumentative conversation. He had been brought up to it from a boy, his father, as I have heard, accustoming his children to dispute with one another for his diversion, while sitting at table after dinner; but I think the practice was not wise; for, in the course of my observation, these disputing, contradicting, and confuting people are generally unfortunate in their affairs. They get victory sometimes, but they never get good will, which would be of more use to them. (P. 733)

Even in his youth, Franklin comprehended the importance of humility and made a deliberate effort to cultivate a style of moderation.

> I made it a rule to forbear all direct contradiction to the sentiments of others, and all positive assertion of my own. I even forbid myself, agreeably to the old laws of our Junto, the use of every word or expression in the language that imported a fix'd opinion, such as *certainly, undoubtedly,* etc., and I adopted, instead of them, *I conceive, I apprehend,* or *I imagine* a thing to be so or so; or it *so appears to me at present.* When another asserted something that I thought an error, I deny'd myself the pleasure of contradicting him abruptly, and of showing immediately some absurdity in his proposition; and in answering I began by observing that in certain cases or circumstances his opinion would be right, but in the present case there *appear'd* or *seem'd* to me some difference, etc. I soon found the advantage of this change in my manner; the conversations I engag'd in went on more pleasantly. The modest way in which I propos'd my opinions procur'd them a readier reception and less contradiction; I had less mortification when I was found to be in the wrong, and I more easily prevail'd with others to give

up their mistakes and join with me when I happened to be in the right.

And this mode, which I at first put on with some violence to natural inclination, became at length so easy, and so habitual to me, that perhaps for these fifty years past no one has ever heard a dogmatical expression escape me. And to this habit (after my character of integrity) I think it principally owing that I had early so much weight with my fellow-citizens when I proposed new institutions, or alterations in the old, and so much influence in public councils when I became a member; for I was but a bad speaker, never eloquent, subject to much hesitation in my choice of words, hardly correct in language, and yet I generally carried my points. (Pp. 632-33)

Franklin concludes that the ability to restrain his own assertiveness was essential to the attainment of his policy ends.

Another common characteristic of the program type exhibited by Franklin is his view of politics as a hobby, as a leisure-time enjoyment secondary to an occupation. In contrast to Bryan, who saw himself giving up a career in law to be "a great man," Franklin saw establishing his printing business, and with it a secure livelihood, as his first task. Public affairs came second to this obligation. In discussing his work remodeling a schoolhouse, Franklin reports,

The care and trouble of agreeing with the workmen, purchasing materials, and superintending the work, fell upon me; and I went thro' it the more cheerfully, as it did not then interfere with my private business, having the year before taken a very able, industrious, and honest partner, Mr. David Hall. (P. 722)

Notice how Franklin refers to public service as something that may "interfere with" the principal responsibility, his occupation.

At the age of forty-two, Franklin retired from active printing work, having turned the business over to a partner. He describes the transition thus:

> When I disengaged myself, as above mentioned, from private business, I flatter'd myself that, by the sufficient tho' moderate fortune I had acquir'd, I had secured leisure during the rest of my life for philosophical studies and amusements. I purchased all Dr. Spence's apparatus, who had come from England to lecture here, and I proceeded in my electrical experiments with great alacrity; but the publick, now considering me as a man of leisure, laid hold of me for their purposes, every part of our civil government, and almost at the same time, imposing some duty upon me. The governor put me into the commission of the peace; the corporation of the city chose me of the common council, and soon after an alderman; and the citizens at large chose me a burgess to represent them in Assembly. (P. 723)

Franklin sees himself entering public life in retirement, when "leisure" had been obtained to pursue personal amusements and hobbies like electrical experiments.

The late entry into politics of program types like Franklin contrasts with the generally early entry of status types. Status types are inclined to see political success as their main career purpose. As a result, they tend to begin their political activity at an early age, usually by their mid-twenties. This difference in entry age of program and status types can be used as an approximate indirect measure for distinguishing between the two types.

Although, as we have indicated, program-incentive themes and orientations predominate in Franklin's autobiography, the work also suggests other incentives. In particular, there are a few comments that suggest a status incentive. At the beginning of the work, for example, Franklin gives his fifth reason for writing: "perhaps I shall a good deal gratify my own *vanity*" (p. 217). Or, to take another instance, in commenting upon his election as an alderman and also as a burgess, Franklin mentions as one of the positive aspects of the posts the appeal of status:

I would not, however, insinuate that my ambition was not flatter'd by all these promotions; it certainly was; for, considering my low beginning, they were great things to me; and they were still more pleasing, as being so many spontaneous testimonies of the public good opinion, and by me entirely unsolicited. (P. 723)

Although such comments indicate an ingredient of status preoccupation in Franklin's makeup, an overall analysis reveals this theme to be a secondary one. First, Franklin's candor in confronting the issue of vanity argues against his being a status type. Status participants, preoccupied with making a good impression, typically attempt to hide the unflattering, self-seeking aspect of their personality. Bryan, the reader will recall, denied being actuated by any motive of self-glorification and attempted to present himself as self-effacing.

A second argument against Franklin's being a status type is the absence from the autobiography of any detailed accounts of struggles for positions. Although Franklin ran in many elections—successfully and unsuccessfully—he does not discuss any of the tactics, strategies, or experiences associated with them. As we have said, position-getting figures prominently in discussion by status types. Franklin's lack of interest in this subject, then, is evidence against his having a status incentive. Program types alone, as we noted in the case of William Hammersmith, are noticeably uninterested in the history and mechanics of personal position getting.

A final argument concerns the relative emphasis of Franklin's writing. All of the status comments, collected together, would fill about two pages; the program material is over twenty times this amount. And it is not from volume alone that we establish the relative emphasis Franklin places on substantive policy. When Franklin discusses a policy subject, he only incidentally reports his own role; his primary interest is the policy itself.

In the picture Franklin gives us of himself, one element seems to be missing. Franklin was a revolutionary leader, a founder of a new country, active in the midst of momentous political changes. Yet, surprisingly, his autobiography fails to treat heroic, idealistic themes. *Liberty, justice, patriotism, democracy:* such grand abstractions are ignored. This omission is, of course, consistent with the picture we have drawn of program types as participants who focus on concrete, practical, issues, and who ignore the symbolic, rhetorical themes.

One consequence of this orientation is that program types seldom project an image of being "ideological" or "idealistic" participants. We noted this point at the beginning of the chapter. Program types, who are deeply concerned with policy, generally appear less committed than, for example, status types, who are not deeply concerned with policy.

Position-taking "idealists" — such as William Jennings Bryan — operate on the abstract, symbolic level. Program types, like Franklin, shun this sphere and stress practical and specific details. "Idealists" take simple, categorical positions; program types are nondogmatic in their approach. "Idealists" strive for the limelight; program types work unobtrusively.

As a result, program types like Franklin are not regarded as "ideological." Paradoxically, their commitment to substantive policy making inhibits the type of behavior that the public regards as revealing a commitment to substantive policy making.

4 The Conviviality Incentive

THE DESIRE TO BE accepted by other people and to engage in harmonious interaction with them is a common human need. All of us feel this impulse to some degree. We enjoy being with others in a social setting. We want others to feel warmly toward us; we want them to value our company. We do not want to be left out, forgotten, or rejected. Anger directed against us makes us feel uncomfortable; a kind word buoys us up.

For some people, this need is particularly strong; they shape their lives around gratifying it. Many formal and informal activities offer an outlet for this need for social acceptance: church organizations, charitable groups, clubs of all kinds, civic and fraternal organizations. And political participation. Politics, after all, is a highly social activity. In politics people meet together and work side by side for common purposes. There is an atmosphere of hearty friendship and courtesy — at least among participants working on the same team. One who is attracted to politics by these social rewards has, in our terms, a conviviality incentive. He has a pronounced need to please others and to be accepted by them.

In the first chapter, we noted that one of the salient stresses encountered in politics is the hostility of others. It is therefore something of a surprise to discover that anyone seeking friendliness should be found in politics at all. Several considerations explain this paradox.

First, conviviality types tend to avoid the higher, more conflict-laden offices. They are most commonly encountered at the local level in smaller communities—town councils, planning boards, school boards—where a harmonious environment is more likely to prevail. Second, conviviality types employ psychological defenses against hostility. They accentuate perceptions of harmony and friendliness and block out or rationalize away hostility. Finally, politics offers, more than most other activities, great opportunities to be helpful to people and to experience their approval. One builds parks for children; one gives raises to public employees; one solves the problems of constituents. From the perspective of the conviviality type, some degree of hostility is bearable as the cost of gaining greater satisfaction from personal approval.

Before we delineate the characteristics of the conviviality type, it is useful to note a common misunderstanding. Terms like "conviviality," "sociability," and "friendliness" suggest an image of a robust, assertive "back-slapper." The conviviality type corresponds poorly to this stereotype. If anything, he tends to be the reverse of this image: there are clear elements of shyness and modesty in the makeup of the conviviality participant.

An understanding of the incentive itself explains this result. People with a pronounced need for social acceptance are highly sensitive to what others may think of them. Hence, they are cautious about imposing themselves in an unfamiliar social setting; they are anxious not to offend or antagonize. Terms such as "back-slapper" or "glad-hander" are somewhat derogatory. They suggest an individual forcing himself on people before they are ready to accept him. The conviviality type, in particular, would avoid such forwardness. One should not, therefore, associate assertive social behavior with conviviality participants. They are generally shy—sometimes extremely so—and never bumptious.

As we have explained, each incentive type is revealed by the emphasis that the subject places on certain aspects of politics.

For the conviviality type, the emphasis is put on convivial interactions and themes related to this area of satisfaction. To illustrate this orientation, we have selected two conviviality-type politicians for closer examination—one as revealed in a personally focused interview, the other as described in his autobiography.

I. Peter Finley: "Satisfaction to Me Comes from Helping People"

Peter Finley is serving his first term as a councilman in the Maine city of Northville. He entered politics at the age of sixty-six after retiring from his post as city housing director.* The dominant theme of the interview with him is participation in friendly relationships. Asked early in the interview for his reaction to being a councilman, Finley draws a parallel with a drinking party:

Q: Have you enjoyed it?
FINLEY: Every minute of it.
Q: Uh-huh.
FINLEY: I've had a ball for myself. I wouldn't dare to give you a quote from a friend of mine. We used to—years back when we were single—fifteen or sixteen of us married and single fellows used to go over to New York to the Army-Notre Dame game. When that stopped, then we used to go to the World Series. Well, most of these fellows are dead now. One fellow always went with us.... It was free, you know, you'd let down and...had a few drinks for yourself, and he would get a few and he would start to laugh, and...I was just going to say the same thing about the city council. I just haven't had, you know, as much honest-to-God fun. I mean, I have a sense of humor.

---

*The name, city, and certain details regarding the official posts of this respondent have been changed to protect his identity.

> Q: Uh-huh.
> FINLEY: If I ever lose that, I'll get off the council.
> Q: Uh-huh.
> FINLEY: And he [the friend] used to be the same way. He'd get about two drinks and he'd say, "I haven't had so much fun since my aunt so-and-so..." You know? So I feel this way. I enjoy fellow councilors. 'Course I know all the department heads, and... I'm just free....

Of all the aspects of council activity — policy making, appearing in public, debating — Finley singles out the camaraderie of the group. Notice that he digresses to reminisce about convivial experiences as a sports spectator. Generally speaking, digressions in an interview have a special significance: they reveal a topic the respondent wants to stress. We see the operation of this rule again in the interview when the subject of education comes up:

> FINLEY: I believe in education. I believe in it. I happen to have two thoughts on education — a Jesuit, St. Thomas Aquinas philosophy.... I went from Holy Cross, which is a Jesuit school, to the C.S.C.s — the Fathers of the Holy Cross at Notre Dame. And when I — and you have to laugh at some of these things — and when I took my language exam, you know, for my master's, you could either take it in a modern language, or you could take either —
> Q: Latin...
> FINLEY: Latin or Greek. So I took it in Latin. So (soft laugh) there's three of them, you know? So they said, "Well, read the Latin." I got about four words out of me and they started to laugh, "Another one of those damn Jesuit students, ohhh." But it was a *friendly* — you know — but the pronunciation, you see, of the Latin from the Jesuits vs. the C.S.C....

Finley drifts away from the topic, educational policy, and inserts an anecdote about a convivial experience that took place over forty years before. He never does return to his "two thoughts on education." Especially interesting is the feature of this event that has so anchored itself in Finley's mind: he is being judged by his superiors. His sense of apprehension and inadequacy is dispelled by the examiners' good-natured joshing about his pronunciation.

The recounting of friendly social experiences, then, reveals a preoccupation with social acceptance. This preoccupation also appears in the stress the respondent gives to being nice, helping people, and sympathizing with their problems:

> FINLEY: I had a reputation of never being, of always being fair with everybody. I never sent anybody out of my office — he might have been damning me at the door — I never sent him out an enemy.
>
> Q: Uh-huh.
>
> FINLEY: 'Cause I would talk with them. I had an open-door policy. Anybody could see me at any time....
>
> I think that the key to the whole thing is that you have, and I've always felt that I've had, a sympathetic understanding of problems — of people's problems, on an individual basis....
>
> I feel like, you know, I listen to people, and — they participate by their input to me, and I take it from there and — and I feel that if I have to get legislation through, or orders or resolutions, and so on and so forth, then I...this is where the satisfaction comes. Satisfaction to me comes from helping people....
>
> Q: Well, it's so very time-consuming, obviously. What do you think attracts people to Maine politics?
>
> FINLEY: I don't know what attracts the other people. I mean, I feel that, you know, I can speak only for myself.
>
> Q: Uh-huh.
>
> FINLEY: I've always been involved with people. I've always been involved in an organization, so I mean...all during my health and housing [career], and being a member of the House of Delegates of the American Housing Association for nine years, almost as long as anybody in the country, and down through the regional and down through the state level, and president of the Maine Housing Association a couple of times, and the Maine Preservation League once, and...I participate.

Finley likes people and values their friendship. His helpfulness elicits the personal support and approval of others. He enjoys congenial interactions. These themes are central in interviews with the conviviality type.

Consistent with the friendship-helpfulness-congeniality pattern of responses is an especially strong dislike of personal conflict, for conflict represents the opposite of personal approval. Above we saw that Finley strove never to send anyone out of his office as an enemy. Several other statements in the interview reinforce the theme of avoiding conflict or being disturbed by it.

For example, shortly before the interview was conducted, the city of Northville had experienced some acrimonious controversies concerning a threatened strike by policemen. Referring to these conflicts, Finley exclaims,

> FINLEY: This is it, this year it's horrifying! It's terrible! Who would ever think that they would — and they can't tell me that, that so-called intelligent, professional people aren't behind them — when you give speeches for kids to read.

Finley continues by citing the case of a fellow councilman who has been attacked:

> FINLEY: I know several instances not only as far as the bank is concerned, but other people that they want to attack. They'll attack...Spruance. You know, these people who are in business — his family in town has a...comes from a grand family, a large bunch of uncles, very close, two or three businesses in town....
> Q: Uh-huh.
> FINLEY: ...and that's a pretty tough cause. Well this...I abhor it. I've gotten out of it.

Naturally, few politicians enjoy conflict, especially controversies involving personal attacks. But conviviality participants are notable for the intensity of their dislike of conflict and for the extensive efforts they make to avoid it.

The conflict surrounding the policemen is atypical of politics in Northville. Finley is by and large comfortable about the politics in his community. In contrast, he views the political scene in faraway Washington, D.C., as being cold and forbidding. For example, he mentions that "the party politics are so, so crummy in Washington." And in discussing one federal agency, he states, "These fellows—the bureaucrats—they can undercut you so fast, it isn't even funny." Finley is content to stay at the local level, and he has no desire to get involved in national politics.

Although he is critical of remote categories of politicians and groups that produce conflict, Finley is reluctant to criticize specific individuals, especially fellow participants in Northville. Indeed, consistent with a common characteristic of conviviality types, he readily and warmly praises other people. Here are some examples:

> We've had exceptionally good men represent the state of Maine. You go back to the Hales; nobody could equal those people. Fred Hale, the senator, and his brother—Robin, I guess—the representative.

> I could point you out men that I always admired. There were two senators from Montana—Wheeler and Walsh. We had outstanding men.

> It was a terrific [WPA] program. And we had two outstanding administrators....

> And he was an outstanding individual, [Robert] Moses.

> [Abraham] Ribicoff, whom I have all the admiration in the world for—in my opinion, one of the greatest men that ever lived.

The obverse of this tendency to praise is the tendency to avoid critical remarks about specific individuals. A negative remark, after all, is the beginning of a conflict. Anxious to avoid starting down the road toward a hostile relationship, the conviviality participant carefully avoids criticism even in a private informal interview.

> Q: Is there anything I might have left out? Any important aspect of your job that I haven't touched on? Or anything you feel you have to say that might help us understand your job?
>
> FINLEY: I think that I would like to, as I said at the beginning, I would like to see... a better representation. I'm not, I'm not going to say nothing against my fellow councilmen, but I would like to see a couple of women running on the council. I would like to see, instead of three lawyers, I would like to see some thirty-, thirty-five, forty-year-age active businessmen, junior executives, or whatever you want to call them. And then you have to have a couple of senior citizens, I suppose, in there, with...
>
> Q: Is there any way you can think of, any ideas you have to make this come about in this city? Some way to, you know, to spark people to run?
>
> FINLEY: Well, I should, this is what I'm in, this is what I'm going to try and do as... as the... as fellows, as the present members no longer run. I'm going to try and... and... I find no fault with my present associates and... but as they, you know, like... they feel like... you know, after all, this year... David Johnson, who's the mayor, is probably one of the swellest fellows, one of the grandest guys you'd ever want to meet, but he's just gone through a crucifixion....

This excerpt betrays a fascinating change of perspective. Finley begins by seeming to find his fellow councilmen inadequate, in need of being retired. Then he spends the rest of the time backtracking on the point. He squarely contradicts himself by saying he finds "no fault" with his colleagues. Why then should he feel the need for "better representation"? Notice that he avoids "better representatives," focusing instead on the formal aspect ("representation"). Finley does not for a moment contemplate actively opposing any of his colleagues in order to bring about a change in membership. Indeed, it appears he can hardly bear the thought of their leaving the council. He stammers and hesitates in contemplating their departure; he cannot even let the simple phrase "as they retire" escape his lips. Finally, he totally reverses himself and starts singing the praises of his fellows, as if distressed by the thought that "one of the grandest guys you'd ever want to meet" might leave his circle of friends.

Another feature of the conviviality type is the self-doubting, self-deprecating tone he adopts in the interview. He appears uncertain of himself (as in the above excerpt), sometimes almost deliberately portraying himself as Caspar Milquetoast. To some extent, this orientation is the outgrowth of his basic insecurity. But self-deprecation is also a functional style: by lowering oneself, one presents a nonaggressive, likable personality.

For example, Finley deliberately refers to himself as an "old fogy."

> FINLEY: I think we [councilmen] have respect for one another.
> Q: Uh-huh.
> FINLEY: No matter how wide apart we may be.
> Q: Uh-huh.
> FINLEY: And I think this is, this is true of this council. We have some young fellows, and we have some middle-aged, and a couple of old fogies like Jackson and myself. See, he was glad I got elected because then he ceased to be the oldest one (laughs).

Elsewhere, Finley stresses his inexperience when asked for his personal reaction to being on the council:

> Q: What has been your most enjoyable experience? (pause) In the council? (pause) What's the most satisfying thing?
> FINLEY: Well, of course, I've only been on a year...about a year and a half. I think it's...I still feel in some respects a little bit of an amateur. I think that.... My first year I sat and listened. I made contributions only in those areas in which I had, probably had, expertise that nobody else had.

Finley hesitates ("probably had") even to claim expertise (in the housing field, where he was city director for many years).

The word "little" is significant. We find this adjective cropping up regularly in conviviality interviews and rarely in interviews with other types. Apparently it fits the conviviality type's need to diminish his claims.

Another feature that is quite common with conviviality interviews and rare in interviews with other types is an expression of concern about the helpfulness of the interview. Conviviality types are anxious on this point: "I hope I've been of use to you in your study" is a common comment. Finley expresses this worry:

> Q: I really appreciate your time. I know it's an awful hot day and you've been...
> FINLEY: I just hope it does—you know, I hope it's what you want. I mean I'm not—I don't want you—I hope it's what you want to hear.
> Q: That's exactly what we want.

Finley practically pleads for reassurance from the interviewer.

Many interviews with conviviality types contain an anomalous element: occasional claims by the respondent that he has stood courageously alone against vigorous opponents. At first, such claims might be interpreted as revealing an obligation incentive. But closer analysis will contradict this interpretation. In the Finley interview, for example, we find the following expression of courage:

> FINLEY: We had the city-manager form of government for many, many years and we've been free of politics.
> Q: Uh-huh.
> FINLEY: But the last two years, I... It seemed to me that they were, that there were some things being made on purely political expediency, as far as I was concerned. It never bothered me as a department head because I absolutely refused to, absolutely refused to let the council... bother me, or the city manager bother me. I had a job to do. I'd been picked as a department head, and he

was going to have confidence in me, or the council was going to have confidence in me, or they could say, "See you later."
Q: Uh-huh.
FINLEY: That's why I had no problem, no fights with any of them.

Here Finley describes himself as a principled man of action, unflinchingly standing up against other politicians. Indeed, if we are to believe him, he put his foot down so resoundingly that politicians far and wide were afraid even to initiate a conflict. We know, from the body of the interview, that Finley is not describing the situation accurately. He is a man who "abhors" conflict, who prizes getting along with people and being helpful. The excerpt itself negates Finley's claim. Any department head who stood up to the council and manager as firmly as he claims he did could hardly have come out of the situation with "no fights."

Why do conviviality types make these unconvincing claims of courageousness? We believe that they are engaging in a kind of "whistling in the dark." A conviviality participant is timid and anxious to avoid conflict. To counter his anxiety, he tries to perceive himself as unafraid of conflict. He attempts to rebut the explicit or implicit criticisms of himself as "cowardly," saying, in effect, "See, I'm not as timid as people think."

In arriving at an incentive classification, the researcher has two jobs. He looks for comments supporting one classification, and he looks for material refuting other possible classifications. In the preceding pages, we have presented material that supports a conviviality classification for Finley. To complete our analysis, it is useful to consider whether Finley might not have another incentive, such as status or program. An inspection of the interview reveals not only a lack of material that would indicate these other incentives, but also several comments that rather directly contradict the hypothesis that Finley has one of these other incentives.

Consider, for example, the following comment:

Q: What aspect of your work on the council have you enjoyed most?

FINLEY: The budget.

Q: The budget. Why is that?

FINLEY: Well, see I... the first trained, educated city manager we had was a gentleman by the name of Lyman Moore.

Q: Uh-huh.

FINLEY: He brought the budget system to us. And this, with very few exceptions, still remains the same. See, he was a graduate of the University of Pennsylvania, Fels Institute.

Q: Uh-huh.

FINLEY: He was trained in... on all the fields.

Q: Uh-huh.

FINLEY: And was an all-around individual, just the same way as today in hospitals you have your administrators in most respects are those with a master's degree in hospital administration, whereas years ago you'd have a doctor, or you'd have a nurse, or you'd have a purchasing agent, or you'd have an auditor moved up. Well, you can see right off the bat your chances of difficulties.

Q: Uh-huh.

FINLEY: Because you have a doctor, with tendencies that lean towards the doctors; and if you get an accountant, you're getting a guy who's leaning towards, "Well, don't spend ninety-eight cents, and you should only be spending ninety-six." Well, this is why in the field of hospitals, and the same thing is so true with trained city managers. I think Tom Schwartz [previous city manager] was out of Fels. I think Bell Watson [current city manager], I think he's out of Michigan, out there.

Q: Uh-huh.

FINLEY: These fellows are all trained. Basically their background being finance. But they have to serve an internship, which is similar to your doctors, similar to your hospital administrators, who come out of the graduate school. He has to do a year of intern — in a hospital. And these fellows have to do a year's intern in the city.

He brought the system here and, to me, it was marvelous. I really enjoyed, I really enjoy budget... and making the budget out so that, so that... I had an exceptionally good secretary, it wasn't all me... exceptionally good secretary at the Housing Department. I handled both budgets — Housing and the city hospital. And she would... I would prepare them and she would type them — always did a good job. And we... I've always, I think... they still hold the Housing and the hospital budgets up as the criterion, the criterion for everybody else to hold.

In the above excerpt, we see the status classification for Finley is negated by the manner in which he places himself below the great minds and "trained" professionals who created the budget system and who manage the city government. The program classification is negated by Finley's drifting away from the substantive issue of budgeting: he avoids policy questions entirely. Hence, even though he says he enjoys making the budget — a policy-making activity — we see that his real interest is not in the substance of policy.

The excerpt also contains further support for the conviviality classification: (1) when Finley drifts away from the subject of budgeting, he drifts to the subject of personalities; (2) Finley warmly praises other individuals; (3) even in credit-claiming, Finley feels the need to diminish his own role ("it wasn't all me").

The rambling, digressive nature of this excerpt — and of the entire Finley interview — is itself another conviviality clue. For other incentive types, an interview is a task: the interviewer has questions, the respondent's job is to answer. For the conviviality type, however, an interview is an opportunity for a friendly interaction. He is likely to ramble and digress about his Aunt Minnie, just as though he were socializing with friends in the neighborhood bar.

II. BROOKS HAYS: "WANTING TO GIVE EVERY STUDENT AN *A*"

Brooks Hays of Arkansas served as a Democrat in the U.S. House of Representatives from 1942 through 1958. He represented Little Rock, and the racial strife that shook the city in the 1950s played a major part in his defeat. A moderate on matters of race, Hays was unseated in the 1958 general election by a last-minute write-in campaign on behalf of Independent Democrat Dale Alford, a segregationist. Hays later taught at Rutgers University and subsequently was a special assistant to President Kennedy.

Before reading Hays's informal autobiography, *A Hotbed of Tranquility*,[1] one might conclude from superficial impressions that he was an obligation type of politician. Although national news reports at the time of his defeat did not contain much in-depth information about Hays as a person, they generally portrayed him as a man of deep convictions who sacrificed his political future for the sake of principle on the civil rights issue.[2]

As always, one must beware of jumping to conclusions about the incentive of a public figure on the basis of superficial reports. The reader who picks up Hays's book with the expectation of hearing about politics from a perspective of a crusader will be quite surprised. Nowhere in his 232 pages does Hays discuss the civil rights issue, or the circumstances surrounding his electoral defeat. This is not to say, of course, that he may not have had strong views on civil rights or that he lacked deep convictions about what is morally right and wrong; a conviviality politician can be highly principled, in certain senses of that term.[3] However, moral convictions are not Hays's central preoccupation.

The distinctive theme of Hays's autobiography is humor. A warm, engaging man, Hays delights in entertaining the reader with anecdotes, jokes, and other humorous material. Although few conviviality participants emphasize humor as much as Hays does, this quality fits in nicely with central conviviality themes such as liking people, gaining their approval, interacting with them in a congenial manner, and minimizing conflict. Early in the book, Hays makes a ringing defense of humor as necessary to preserve "companionship":

> In this imperfect world of ours, the strains and stresses of life could destroy man's happiness if he lacked the quality of humor. Politics is one of the great sources of tensions. Humor can become a cohesive force, and laughter a healing exercise; and in this decade [the 1960s] of civil strife and serious problems beyond the seas, when frustration engenders bitterness and passions arise, this precious quality of humor may be our saving grace. It may strengthen our faith and enable us to enjoy companionship, even with those who are on opposing sides. If this volume should be an influence, however feeble, to the realization of this hope, I shall be very happy. (P. 3)

Hays's autobiography is a loosely structured work that meets the three criteria (discussed in chapter 2) for being considered a personally focused, incentive-relevant autobiography. First, the book departs from a chronological presentation at many points. For example, only in the second half of the book does Hays relate some of the experiences of his youth; and even here the material is introduced almost as a series of flashbacks that are incidental to the book as a whole. Second, this autobiography seems to be written from memory. The purpose is to entertain, not to produce a historical record; systematic notes or other documents are not the basis of the narration. Third, the book's topics have an idiosyncratic appearance. Institutions, individuals, and events are discussed insofar as they allow the author to reminisce or tell relevant stories—not in proportion to the historical importance of the topics.

Throughout the autobiography, Hays reveals the conviviality trait of liking people. He makes numerous references to his friendly feelings for others. At the end of one campaign, he refers to "friendships cemented by our struggles and sacrifices" (p. 47). Regarding a House colleague, he claims, "We were warm friends" (p. 85). He describes a senator as "one of my good friends in the Congress" (p. 123), and a judge as the person "whose friendship meant most to me as a young man" (p. 146). He "became very fond" of a German newsman (p. 217); he had a "long and intimate friendship" with Adlai Stevenson (p. 230); he had a "special kind of feeling" for rural people (p. 140). Regarding John F. Kennedy, Hays says:

> My feeling for President Kennedy was not only one of admiration but of affection. Our friendship ripened before he became President, and when I went to the White House as one of his special assistants we had established a congeniality that made it one of the most pleasant assignments my long political service had ever provided. (P. 118)

Hays clearly enjoys helping other people. He recalls that during the Depression he received "one of the most welcome and gratifying telephone calls of my entire life" (p. 156) from Secretary of Labor Frances Perkins:

> She asked me to serve as legal adviser in the Arkansas office of NRA, and at last I found myself in the type of work for which I was temperamentally fitted—work for and with *people*.... [N]ow with the opportunity to work with both management and labor to elevate the status of the Arkansas wage worker, I had found my element. (P. 157)

Hays's personality is also suited to his later experience as a teacher:

> Student contacts are exhilarating. These college assignments have not only given me a lot of pleasure but have provided outlets for my desire to help students who are interested in political careers. (P. 195)

Hays's conception of the teaching role is profoundly revealing of his impulse to help others. The following discussion of assigning student grades shows how Hays perceives his role:

President Johnson took an interest in my excursion into academia, indicating that he would enjoy returning to San Marcos, Texas, college campus which he loved as an undergraduate. If he does, he would very likely have the same problem that I have, wanting to give every student an A. That's the politician in us. I related to the President the incident of the finest apple-polishing job I ever heard of by a student. At the bottom of the examination paper was this personal message, "Professor Hays, I am not proud of my performance on this examination. It does not meet my standards, but you see I was up all night. At six o'clock this morning, my wife gave birth to a little girl. I was so disappointed! I wanted a boy. I intended to name him for you." A-plus was the best I could do for him!

I can sympathize with those who are responsible for establishing the measurements for excellence. Still, gradations of progress can be fairly uniform. It has been discovered in a survey of law school graduates, for example, for a period which included my senior year, that the A students are still there; they are teaching. The B students are practicing law and are a credit to the profession. The C students are making money in business, and the D students are in Congress.

Currently, this matter of grades engages some good professional minds. I like what one critic of present indexes advances—the idea of *sine laude* honors. If "with honors" is a proper reward, and it certainly is, we ought to work out something for the lads at the bottom who barely make it, not because they don't try, but because being far below number two they have to try harder just to stay in the game! Life in this transitory vale of tears will never find us mortals distributing rewards and honors with perfect justice. We should, however, seek an approximation of it. (P. 187)

The dominant orientation of this passage is being kind to others: Hays even equates justice with kindness. He describes his own impulse, as a teacher and as a politician, as one of wanting to be nice to everyone. He makes the assumption, through self-projection, that all politicians are philanthropists by nature. He is dimly aware of the need for academic standards, but leaves the responsibility of asserting them (by unkindly giving low grades) to others.

The second paragraph of the above excerpt rambles off the point, illustrating the conviviality type's tendency to digress. The digression itself displays another conviviality indication, self-deprecation: Hays, the congressman, is a D student. To ingratiate himself, Hays is willing to ridicule himself and his profession.

One of the prominent themes in Hays's book is his thorough enjoyment of harmonious, congenial interactions with other people. He takes fully two pages to recount some convivial banter with President and Mrs. Eisenhower during a dinner in 1966 (pp. 107-8). In discussing Congress, Hays stresses the warmth and good feelings found in the cloakrooms — hardly the most weighty aspect of Congress he might have chosen to emphasize:

> If the congressional committees are the heart of congressional activities, the camaraderie of the cloakroom must be the soul. The cloakroom is the one place where the congressional brethren may gather, away from the public eye. These are actual rooms. Each chamber has two spacious clublike lounges, one for the Republicans and one for Democrats, immediately off the actual formal chambers, where they can let their hair down. The easy informality of the cloakroom exchanges mitigates the personal and sometimes bitter clashes on the floor. One might even be jerked out of mental depression by the frolicsome talk of statesmen who are first of all human beings, and almost invariably these humans are universally articulate. The cloakroom invariably leads to relaxation, and relaxation ultimately has to lead to horseplay and humor.
>
> When I came to the House, I wanted to be a member of the "Lodge" and I didn't want to pretend to be a member until I had really been admitted. Somewhere along the line I apparently acquired a reputation as a good storyteller. Deserved or undeserved, it was pretty firm, and this was a great advantage. (P. 84)
>
> In the cloakroom the harshness that often creeps into official debates is abandoned, ribbing is good-natured, and the laughter that follows personal thrusts is untinged with malice. Even when

the philosophical cleavages are sharp, such as those between the Virginia Conservative, Judge Howard Smith, and hard-hitting left-winger, the late Vito Marcantonio of New York, the off-the-floor give and take is pleasant and often witty. Marcantonio could always get a chuckle from colleagues by his threat to go into Virginia to campaign for Judge Smith by saying nice things about him at every stop.

Judge Smith would get into the spirit of the game and say coaxingly, "You wouldn't treat me like that, now would you, Marc? You're much too kind a man!"

Underneath the badinage, there was considerable respect for each other, despite the vast difference in their political philosophies. (P. 73)

Even in describing apparent enemies—Smith and Marcantonio—Hays insists on perceiving friendship and harmony: the men had "considerable respect for each other." Another interpretation would be that the badinage was a veneer that masked a profound hostility between the two men. But a conviviality type like Hays would resist such an interpretation. In the world of the conviviality participant, conflicts are superficial; no one really dislikes anyone.

Hays's aversion to conflict and hostility is revealed in many ways throughout the book. He never criticizes anyone; instead he compliments and praises one figure after another. Even political opponents, Republicans, are treated cordially: Calvin Coolidge "possessed a quiet but deep and wholesome sense of humor" (p. 92); "I admired Mr. Hoover" (p. 95); "Warren G. Harding loved to make people happy by joining their clubs and lodges and fraternities" (p. 97). Significantly, in discussing and praising presidents and other leaders, Hays focuses on their personal friendliness. Other aspects, such as their policy views or their management of their office, he ignores.

The complete lack of policy discussion in the book is another indication of Hays's impulse to avoid conflict. Conviviality types are not deeply interested in policy to begin with; therefore, they will not normally dwell on the subject at any length. But Hays seems to go further, virtually suppressing all mention of issues. Any policy discussion would, of course, introduce a divisive note. Readers would begin taking sides, against Hays or against some of the many people he has such affection for. By eliminating policy discussion altogether, Hays maintains a tone of pure, universal friendliness.

Another conviviality trait, that of self-deprecation, is amply illustrated in the book. For example, Hays calls his early legal career "undistinguished" (p. 144). He speaks of "the vicissitudes and triumphs (yes, there were a few) of my forty years in public service" (p. 185). And he states, "Without aspiring to expertness I have nevertheless made a mild claim to being a multi-specialist..." (p. 185). He is aware that by making fun of himself, he can ingratiate himself with his audience; in discussing political campaigning, he observes, "A joke told by the speaker on himself... never fails to receive an appreciative response" (p. 5).

The following excerpt is a good illustration of Hays's self-effacing character and his extreme reluctance to offend others:

> I remember the time I made my maiden speech in the House. There is a tradition in Congress that new members should be seen and not heard, but after several months I finally got up enough courage to address the speaker, and I spoke for five minutes. The next morning I was too impatient to wait for the *Congressional Record* to be delivered, so I hurried down to the basement of the Capitol to the record clerk's office to pick up a copy. To my great disappointment and utter disgust I found my speech attributed to my good friend, Congressman Oren Harris, also of Arkansas. There it was, just as I had delivered it, but Mr. Harris got the credit! I raced into the Record Clerk's office and told him what I thought of that kind of mistake. I was disappointed and irritated, and could not avoid showing it. Then I suddenly realized that I was completely out of character, and making too much of what was

really an unimportant matter. I had gotten along well with the staff and wanted the happy relationship to continue. So I apologized and said, "Forgive me. Why, of course, I shouldn't have said anything about it. We all make mistakes. It was understandable." He said cheerfully, "Oh, that's all right, Mr. Hays. You should have heard Mr. Harris." (P. 76)

In another passage Hays describes his timidity:

One can never entirely lose the feeling of awe in the presence of an American President. Even in later years—beginning with Mr. Roosevelt's administration in 1933, when my service on the Democratic National Committee and in the Congress produced invitations to many social events in the White House—I had a self-consciousness that fortunately operated as a brake on my conversational proclivities. I have an embarrassing recollection of an occasion when President Roosevelt invited seventy freshmen congressmen of both parties to the White House. Afterward Joe Martin told Charlie Halleck, the President shed so much charm it would take a month for the Republicans to come out of the ether.

As we gathered around President Roosevelt, Speaker Sam Rayburn gave me a push toward a chair on the President's left, and whispered, "You sit down there, Brooks." Taking thankfully what the gods provided, I slid into the vacant chair, just as the President began to speak.

It was an informal occasion, and when presently he said something I agreed with, I said, "That's right."

He whizzed around, leaning slightly forward in his chair. His eyes, only about a foot away, looked right into mine. "How's that?" he said.

My self-consciousness, forgotten for a moment, returned in a rush. "That's right," I repeated feebly. He looked pleased, jerked his head up and down twice, and ejaculated, "Yeh!"

The next day I was the butt of the badinage that normally goes on in the cloakroom. Those who weren't there were regaled with the story of how the greatest living man turned to their colleague with a question, gave him the floor, and paused along with a waiting world for words of wisdom to issue from his lips! And what happened? In a tone so low it was hardly above a whisper, like a fizzling fuse, their colleague from Arkansas had murmured, "That's right." (Pp. 91-92)

Anyone who thinks that all politicians are basically alike should try to imagine William Jennings Bryan writing this passage! Even assuming Bryan might have had such an experience, it is unlikely that he would remember it—let alone report it—in such a self-deprecatory way.

The above passage also illustrates the passive orientation of the conviviality type. These participants tend to view themselves as observers or spectators rather than active, central participants. We see this orientation in the incident with Roosevelt. Hays momentarily lapses into an active role and then, embarrassed to be the center of attention, retreats back into the audience.

The autobiography concentrates much more on the activities of other politicians than on situations in which Hays is the main focus of attention. For example, the chapter on Congress contains, by our count, fifty-five anecdotes; in only sixteen of these is Hays the principal actor—often the butt of some joke or embarrassment. His acceptance of the role of passive observer is especially evident in his discussion of recent American presidents. Here he is not only a spectator but also one who reports being awed by those he is observing. He is thrilled at signs of recognition and acceptance by great men. For example, he says that one of his "prized possessions" is a congratulatory postcard from Adlai Stevenson, one of his personal heroes.

Hays's spectator orientation is nicely illustrated in his description of his first reaction to Washington:

> One of my constituents, an Arkansas farmer who saved his money to pay a visit to the city his taxes had helped build, wanted to see the Capitol and the White House. In the Capitol he got into a restricted zone, and an insensitive guard, probably new and uninstructed, waved him back rather abruptly.

"Get back there! Who do you think you are anyway?"
My friend from Arkansas controlled his feelings. "Nobody," he answered mildly. "Nobody much. Just one of the owners."

In 1919 my attitude toward my capital city was one of awe, not brashness; I had none of the proprietary feeling that the perceptive Arkansas farmer had. Rather, the city overwhelmed me. (P. 89)

In addition to the spectator and timidity themes, this passage illustrates two other conviviality traits. First, there is self-deprecation: Hays places himself below the "perceptive" Arkansas farmer. Second, there is the imputation of friendliness to others. The guard isn't really insensitive, he is "probably new and uninstructed."

From the foregoing description of the conviviality type, it is easy to see why the public image of these participants is generally rather faint and colorless. They avoid placing themselves at the center of the conflicts; they are embarrassed by the limelight of publicity. Many are uneasy about public speaking; they feel more comfortable in the cloakrooms. Hays, of course, received some national publicity owing to his electoral defeat on the race issue. Even so, he was not a widely known figure—and he did not aspire to be. He sought the social acceptance and camaraderie of his colleagues, not the bright but harsh light of public recognition.

5 The Obligation Incentive

FOR THOSE OF US who have been "roped into" coaching Little League, organizing Brownies, or collecting for cerebral palsy, the motivation of "doing one's duty" is quite familiar. We wanted those free evenings and we did not look forward to serving, but we felt that we could not, in good conscience, say no. Someone, we reflected, should undertake these worthy tasks: what right did we have to shove the burden off on someone else? In a mild way, then, many of us have felt the tug of what we call the obligation incentive: the need to follow one's conscience, to engage in correct behavior.

It is not surprising that this drive is an important one in motivating political participation. For those personalities highly responsive to moral imperatives, politics affords a wide range of impelling duties. There is the duty to fight for right policies and oppose wrong ones; the duty to work in behalf of virtuous candidates and work against wicked ones; the duty to stand up for what is legal, fair, or democratic; the duty to resist and expose underhanded and immoral practices; and, of course, there is the duty to serve one's community, state, or nation.

Whether or not politics is viewed as a realm laden with obligations depends, however, on the individual. Most people are not particularly troubled by questions of conscience. They acknowledge that there are issues of right and wrong, but moral imperatives do not dominate their thinking.

On the other hand, there are some political participants who are especially preoccupied about the moral or ethical aspects of political life. It is almost as if they were wearing special glasses that converted all choices and actions into issues of right and wrong. Something inside prompts them to ask, at every turn, "Is it the right thing to do?"

It is this stress on issues of conscience, on the should-ought perspective, that characterizes the obligation type. All politicians, of course, refer now and again to principles of duty and rectitude; they will readily voice the opinion that one should follow one's conscience and do the "right" thing. What sets the obligation type apart is the pervasive, relentless character of his ethical concern. For him, "ought" seems to be the only thing that matters in politics. Or, to express it as he would put it, the inner guide of conscience is the only thing that ought to matter.

"Duty" is the positive way to refer to this type of motive; that is, we can say that the individual seeks to do the right thing. But the same drive can be expressed as a negative orientation: guilt avoidance. We could say the obligation participant seeks to avoid the guilt feeling that he would have if he failed to do the right thing. In a sense, duty and guilt are two sides of the same coin.

In practice, however, we find that obligation types differ in the degree to which they exhibit what one might call guilt anxieties. The two politicians we have selected for our exposition of the obligation incentive exhibit a clear contrast on this point. For our second subject, Frederick L. Hackenburg, guilt feelings figure quite prominently. He portrays himself as tormented by anxieties over having done wrong or having failed to do right. Our first subject, to whom we now turn, expresses no such anxieties. He is preoccupied with issues of right and wrong. He looks at the world through the thick lenses of the moralist. But he is not inclined to accuse himself of failing to live up to moral standards.

I. Armand Dupuis:
"So Maybe I'm Not a Politician"

Armand Dupuis is a vigorous man in his early fifties. He is a popular, well-known mason in Fall River, Maine, a typical New England mill city.* At the time of the interview, he was completing his fourth year as a member of Fall River's city council. Like many inhabitants of Fall River, Dupuis is of French-Canadian descent. He speaks with a slight accent and occasionally struggles for the right word in English. Not having finished high school, Dupuis understandably regrets his lack of formal education. But he defers to no one in speaking his mind.

As we noted above, the salient characteristic of an interview with an obligation participant is the stress on acting rightly. Almost at the beginning of the interview, we find Dupuis launching into this type of material:

> Q: If there was a particular thing that you really were interested in, like say, for instance, maybe keeping industry out, or something like that, or something that you really felt strongly about, how would you go about getting it accepted or adopted by the town council or by the mayor, or whatever?
>
> DUPUIS: Well, first off, there's one thing that you have to remember. In the city of Fall River there's eleven councilmen. I represent one vote. Now, the thing is, a real politician, this is the way they play, but, uh, for some reason I must not be a politician. I cannot support somebody else's bills if I don't believe in it. I mean, I cannot say, "Well, look, I'll support your bill if you support mine." I cannot do this.
>
> Q: Uh-huh.
>
> DUPUIS: So maybe I'm not a politician, I don't know, but I can't do this. If I feel this man will say that he wants a new street or side-

---

*The name and town of the respondent have been changed to protect his identity.

walk, and I feel that the person—where he lives or what, whatever street that he wants—it's necessary, I'll go along a hundred percent with it. But if I feel that the only way that he'll vote for me on a certain thing—that, well, if you vote for me I'll vote for you—I can't go along with that. I'll vote against it and I'll take my chances. Maybe this is why on the council I have been losing all the time—seven to four, six to five—but I can't play ball. I might be wrong, but I just can't do it.

In addition to expressing the basic obligation theme of sticking to one's beliefs and not "going along," this excerpt reveals two other obligation characteristics. Obligation types, almost universally, are reluctant to apply the term "politician" to themselves. They make a point of insisting that they are different from the usual politician, who is accommodating, pliant, not committed to the defense of principle. In the interview, Dupuis makes six separate, unsolicited claims to not being a "politician."

A second perspective of the obligation type revealed in the above excerpt is the theme of aloneness, of going against the tide (and down to defeat) as a consequence of following one's inner standards. Notice that Dupuis does not give an intellectual defense of his conduct. He reports it as simply against his nature to "play ball." We can almost believe that he would like, on occasion, to wheel and deal. But the construction of his personality will not allow him to put his convictions aside.

We get a fuller picture of the pervasive, relentless character of Dupuis's moralistic approach to all topics in the following excerpt. He begins by objecting, on principle, to the practice of increasing salaries after the budget for the year has been approved. But then he wanders onto several other topics, always stressing right and wrong.

> DUPUIS: .... So they changed a few items, you know: one guy they gave him a thousand-dollar raise; the next man, Parks and

Recreation, they gave him a nine-hundred dollar raise, but in this budget it was five hundred dollars; and we'll say there was a difference about, for department heads, we'll say about three or four thousand dollars.

Q: Uh-huh.

DUPUIS: But that ain't the point. The point is the budget was for four million, nine hundred; now it's four million, nine hundred — *allons* more! Yet they [other councilmen] accept the budget of four million, nine hundred and so, which is wrong.

Q: Uh-huh.

DUPUIS: And I voted against this. But like I said, the vote was nine to two. For some reason, I don't know, you can't reach these people. But they're tremendous workers, though, I mean. But like I said, they've been, I think they've been in office for too long. Without hurting my fellow councilmen — there's eleven of us — and you get about six of them they're workers. The rest of them, well they've been there, and there's one of 'em been there for almost twenty years, you know, he just relaxes. He never goes to committee meetings. And this is wrong. And there's another thing I don't like —

Q: (interrupts) Be as candid as you want, because it's strictly confidential, let me just reassure you.

DUPUIS: (talking over the interviewer) No, no. There's another thing. I'm a registered Democrat, and if there's a Republican person running, I don't care what ticket he's on, or Independent, and if I feel that this person is qualified, I will vote for this person, and I will fight for this person.

Q: So that you don't vote just for the party, you vote for the man?

DUPUIS: I vote for the man. However, there are some.... Fall River, especially Fall River, 80 percent of Fall River will vote for the party. This is wrong. They should have a two-party system here.

Word choice alone points up Dupuis' relentless preoccupation with rectitude. He uses the words "should" and "ought" throughout; sixteen times in the interview he declares that something "is wrong."

When asked about desirable qualities in a politician, Dupuis first mentions "education," but he does not elaborate. Instead, he stresses the qualities most valued by obligation participants — integrity and following one's conscience:

> Q: Perhaps we've touched on this a little bit. I just wondered, what qualities do you think it takes to make a good councilman? I mean, you have mentioned education and things like that, but what... (trails off)
>
> DUPUIS: Well, first off, the first and most important thing, it's education. Secondly, I think, it's honesty.
>
> Q: Uh-huh.
>
> DUPUIS: You can't be prejudiced. I mean, my uncle could come up there and try to do.... Well, I'm a councilman, I'm a city father, I make the law. Well, you know, I can open a lot of doors, or go see the chief here, the chief there, or the building inspector, or something like that. I think you should be honest. If there's an ordinance, this is against the law, it's against the law, regardless if he's your cousin, your brother.... To me this is the nicest quality that a councilman would have. 'Cause they make the law and they should obey the law. Uh, thirdly, a man... it's all right to be friends with his fellow councilmen, with the mayor and everything, 'cause he ran with the party and, you know, political campaign. However, he should vote the way that he feels it's right. I mean, me, I vote what my conscience tells me. All right, there's a lot of times that I'm not sure, quite sure, then I'll hear the arguments on both sides, and I'm still not decided, you know? But you still have to vote. You cannot, you can't excuse; you have to vote.

Notice that Dupuis, at the end of the above excerpt, puts following his conscience ahead of other considerations, even information-gathering. Only when the voice of his conscience is muted does he see himself listening to "arguments on both sides." This dogmatic perspective is revealed even more clearly as the interview continues:

Q: It's better... you say it would be better to be right than to win? You'd be better off to be right than to win?
DUPUIS: Oh yes, definitely, 'cause winning—hey, I don't care about winning.
Q: Uh-huh.
DUPUIS: I feel if you come in front of me and you have a problem, I'll listen to your problem. However, a lot of people come in front of you, they got problem 'cause they want to get around their little problem—it's their fault. Now if I feel that it's solvable, it's really a problem and I can solve it, I would help this person to solve this. However, my fellow councilmen might not agree with me. They'll say, well it's going to cost the city money for this. But regardless what they say—if I feel that I can help this person, I will help him. Once I make up my mind, I never change.

Although at many points in the interview Dupuis stresses the importance of "common sense," it is clear that he is not a pragmatist. For him, common sense does not mean responding to practical considerations, or yielding to the prevailing view. Common sense is doing what he believes "way down deep there" is right.

DUPUIS: Thing is, it's not always education. To me, you know—they talk about education, they say it's wonderful—but I think the most precious thing for any man in office is common sense.
Q: Hm.
DUPUIS: To me, it's common sense. I mean, I can listen to them talk all night: "We're gonna do this, we're gonna do that." They use big words that... but way down deep there, if you don't use common sense, it's no good.
Q: Uh-huh.
DUPUIS: I've seen a lot of college boys—we've got plenty around here—and I talk to them, you know. To me, [an idea] sounds silly; to them, it's wonderful. They think they know everything. I'm not against college, I wish I could have went to college, you know. But if you don't have common sense—forget it.

Later in the interview, Dupuis explicitly equates common sense with following his conscience:

> DUPUIS: [The mayor is] really a politician. Him, he loves it. I mean, let's face it, me, I'm not a politician. I, I vote what I believe is right, common sense. That's it.

On policy issues, obligation types express firm, dogmatic positions on a wide range of subjects. But their discussions are one-sided and not comprehensive. They appear to believe that their position is the only correct one, a moral imperative. In this respect, obligation participants are quite unlike program types, who are open-minded and empirical in their approach to policy questions.

In the course of the interview, Dupuis skips through a large number of policy points, offering his one-sided, rigid view on each: city growth and industrial development, revenue sharing, city land purchases, welfare, public housing, zoning, subsoil tests for commercial property. The following remarks on the local leash law are typical of his dogmatic (excuse the pun) approach:

> DUPUIS: I always vote against the leash law, but yet all over the state they are for the dog license, you know, leash law.
> Q: Hm.
> DUPUIS: All right, I'm against it for one reason. Now they took away the poll tax, I'm paying five dollars for my dog: he's got more rights on the street than the people of Fall River, as far as I'm concerned.
> Q: Uh-huh.
> DUPUIS: Now I say if you want to have a leash law, all right: let's all the citizens of Fall River don't pay taxes for their dog. Then they can put 'em on a leash.
> Q: Uh-huh.
> DUPUIS: Oh, you can't do this. You mean to tell me I gotta pay five dollars for my dog, and I gotta tie him up? That's not pleasant.
> Q: Uh-huh.

DUPUIS: Suppose you don't like a dog, but you happen to like a cat. Suppose my dog runs after your cat, what would you do? Throw a rock at my dog, wouldn't you, huh?

Q: Uh-huh.

DUPUIS: So you don't like dogs — all right. But some people love dogs, some people love cats, some people's got canary birds — all kinds of pets. How many people in the city of Fall River have pets, any kind of pet, whether it's a bird, cats, or dog? Now, if I'm going to pay five dollars for my dog, and these people, they're not paying any taxes at all, why, why should I tie him up? You know? (continues on the same point)

In Dupuis's eyes, the leash law question is a simple question of right and wrong, of equal treatment for dogs. That cats and canaries act differently and with different social consequences does not seem to enter his mind.

Unlike conviviality participants, obligation types are quite unconcerned with personal warmth and approval. They follow their inner standards of right and wrong and are unmindful of giving offense. Indeed, obligation types often see popularity seeking as pernicious. The politician who seeks popular approval will be forced, they believe, to depart from frank, upright conduct. Dupuis expresses this theme in the following comment when he is asked if he might want to be mayor:

DUPUIS: I think to run a city, to be a good mayor — I don't think a person should be loved. But over here, like I told you before, in Fall River, it's how popular you are. But I think to be a good mayor you gotta be straight.

Elsewhere, Dupuis expresses his attitude toward constituents who ask for favors on the basis of their past or potential electoral support:

DUPUIS: ...and this is being done today too much. And too much political pull: "Hey, look, I voted for you the last time." Me, I don't care. Look [as if replying to a constituent] I'm doing the job. If you don't like the way I'm doing the job, next year don't vote for me. I'm a councilman, all right. If I'm not a councilman, it's still all right. I think I'm doing the city a favor. I really am, for what I'm being paid.

Q: Uh-huh.

DUPUIS: But people are not like that. They say, "Well look," — we'll say the American Legion — "Hey look, if we don't have this then we won't support you." Look, if you don't support me, okay; if you do, all right. You know, that's the way I feel, so.... Maybe I'm wrong. Like I said, maybe I'm not a politician, but that's the way I feel.

As the above comment illustrates, not all elected officials are anxious to curry favor with their constituents. Status and conviviality types may, to a degree, conform to this popular stereotype. Confronted by constituent demands, the normal orientation of these types is to be sympathetic, regardless of what the popular demands might be.

The obligation type contradicts this image. He is, by nature, a trustee. Citizens, he agrees, have a right to petition him. But if he disagrees with them, his conscience will lead him not only to behave oppositely, but probably to tell them off as well. Many politicians may be swayed by threats of electoral reprisal, but not the obligation type. He is particularly immune to considerations of popularity or electoral success.

II. FREDERICK L. HACKENBURG: "A STRAIGHT AND NARROW PATH"

What was it like to combat the Democratic party organization in New York City in the heyday of machine politics? An illuminating account of such a challenge, by the man who made it, is Frederick L. Hackenburg's autobiography, *A Solitary Parade*.[1] Hackenburg was a Czech immigrant who came to New York in 1904, at the age of sixteen. There is much of Horatio Alger in his story. He began penniless and friendless in his newly adopted land and had to work at menial jobs. Later, by studying on his own, he obtained the New York Regent's certificate and entered law school. At the age of twenty-eight, he was admitted to the New York Bar.

Hackenburg was a political reformer, a crusader for purity in politics. A status type might adopt a crusading stance with little interest in the policies themselves. But Hackenburg was deeply committed to the measures he advocated. He subordinated egocentric needs to higher principles, to following conscience and the path of duty. His story is a classic portrait of the obligation participant in politics.

Obligation types report their entry into politics as motivated by their sense of citizen duty. They enter politics not for positive satisfactions, but in response to an ethical imperative that the situation forces upon them. For Hackenburg, the circumstance that provoked his conscience was the corruption of the New York City Democratic machine. As he describes it,

> The local organization had drifted into the hands of a few selfish and irresponsible individuals, who traded on the reputation of those who built before them. The controlling clique was intoxicated with power. Nominations, appointments and contracts went to their relatives and business associates, often for a consideration. The clubhouses became asylums for political chair-warmers, useless drones and petty schemers. Everybody wanted something without giving anything in return. Nepotism, graft, greed were in the air; disregard of popular rights and interests lurked everywhere.
>
> The machine, bulky, arrogant, threatening, was irresponsive to popular touch.
>
> It had outlived its usefulness. It had no mission to perform and no purpose to serve; it was ready to be scrapped. But there was no deliverer in sight. People felt the situation; unfortunately they were either busy with their own affairs, or indifferent to the whole scheme of things, or afraid to stir for fear of vengeance from the politicians in power. (Pp. 47-48)

Hackenburg saw a wrong that others, consulting their own personal convenience and safety, refused to combat. But

Hackenburg could not so easily shirk his duty. His conscience would not leave him alone:

> I felt restless and humiliated whenever my mind dwelt on the local political situation. As the months passed there slowly ripened in my mind a determination to do something about it. I delved into the provisions of the Election Law and studied the recent amendments to it....
>
> There was no direct primary than and to ask for the floor at a party convention without being first officially designated by the local leader for that honor and distinction, was akin to an attempt to swim up the Niagara falls. The local conventions were packed with ward heelers and worse. Blackjacks were in readiness to supplement the gavel.
>
> Still the thing worried me; I felt a strong urge to do something about it.
>
> I spent several hectic evenings discussing the matter with [a close friend]. After long consideration of the subject we arrived at the conclusion that there was nothing wrong with democracy. All it needed was the additional application of more democracy. The problem reduced itself to one of civic education.
>
> One Sunday morning we called together a handful of the boys from the neighborhood corners to a meeting in the local settlement and organized a kind of debating club along civic lines for the discussion of vital current problems of a political nature.
>
> This was a most unusual way to attempt to enter local politics. However, soon we formed a compact, interested, aggressive group. (Pp. 52-53).

After some initial reverses, Hackenburg's Democratic reform club, the Yorkville Civic Forum (founded in 1912), was finally successful in electing its man, Thomas Farley, to the post of New York City alderman. After this victory, Hackenburg weighed the desirability of quitting politics:

> A small inner voice in the innermost recesses of my soul urged me to quit the political game at this stage. Our initial battle was

fought, I had had a good stiff smell of the powder, and I had proven that if Tammany Hall is a feudalism, it can be tempered by primaries.

I saw the drawbacks of association; a dyer's hand becomes black as the result of his trade. I had an honorable profession, youth, good health and the smiling wide world before me. I knew enough about practical politics to draw back somewhat when it came to the function of dealing out the loaves and fishes to a constituency. I was in a position to earn a livelihood in my practice of law. I shrank back from a political income. I knew of the prevalence of graft, and of the attitude of the average adept in politics. A story is told about General Bluecher, who by his timely arrival at Waterloo turned the tide of the battle and brought about Napoleon's final downfall. He came to London after his victory, was feted and shown around the immense metropolis. They took him to the top of St. Paul's and pointed out the great spreading town below. The comment of the Prussian cavalry leader was characteristic: "What a city to loot!"

The average politician has the true Bluecherian attitude. I was averse to acquiring this state of mind.

At the same time I liked the game. I had tasted victory and was hungry for further battles. I had a desire to build up a real Democratic organization in my district, one that would be responsive to the popular touch. I felt that, with the material we had at hand, we could set an example to the rest of the city. The past was closed and we were facing legitimate success and could follow a straight and narrow path to goals worth while.

Anyhow, I persuaded myself. I desired the activity and activity I got. (Pp. 90-91)

For Hackenburg the arguments on both sides of the decision to remain in politics are ethical ones. If he were to stay in politics, he would associate with corrupt individuals and possibly be corrupted himself; if he quit, he would lose the opportunity to "set an example."

Hackenburg himself neither sought nor took any public office during the first eight years of his political activity. He was offered the post of deputy district attorney by Democratic leader John Coggey, but he turned it down:

> Mr. Coggey stopped for a while to let the weight of the offer sink fully into my mind. I wondered what he was thinking during the short silence. Perhaps he saw the handwriting on the wall and visualized the mighty shaking of dry bones in the fat places on the old payroll.
>
> Quickly, I made my decision. I had fought my way into the sphere of politics. My fight was for a principle. I had no desire to become a shield bearer to anyone. Acceptance meant political bondage.
>
> I refused to be tempted; politely and with profuse thanks I declined the offer. I was going to devote myself to my law practice. And priggishly I quoted Jefferson: "Whenever a man casts a longing eye on an office a rottenness begins in his conduct." (The quotation was in bad taste, and I could readily have refrained from making the remark; unfortunately, tolerance comes only with the experience of reverses and buffeting.) (P. 114)

This excerpt illustrates the obligation type's stress on rectitude. It also shows the dogmatic, offense-giving tendency of this type. Obligation participants are often so obsessed with their black-white world view that they are insensitive to the feelings and perspectives of others. Though Hackenburg is aware, in retrospect, of his "bad taste" in throwing the Jefferson quote in Coggey's face, there is little sign that "buffeting" has made him more tolerant. As we shall note below, Hackenburg's autobiography is remarkable in the extreme degree of dogmatism and intolerance it exhibits.

In 1920, at the age of thirty-two, Hackenburg became the nominee for a State Assembly seat. He describes how the nomination came about and his reaction to it in these words:

> It was a sultry, hot damp night in July, just about the time when district clubhouses become busy with the annual task of gathering the necessary signatures to the nominating petitions.

> Walking into the clubhouse rather later than my usual hour, I was stopped at the door and told that I was wanted upstairs where Farley, since his accession to the leadership, had established his office.
> On his desk were piled up the blank nominating petitions. We discussed the preparation and the circulation of them for a few moments. In a matter-of-course, business-like voice, he added, as if it were a matter of every day routine: "Put your name down as the candidate for the Assembly."
> It was my understanding that another man had been selected as the candidate for that office. I looked at Farley and inquired: "How about Flood?" I was informed that Flood had to undergo a serious operation because of injuries received during the war on the battlefields of France, and that he expected to spend the winter months in hospitals.
> Silently I picked up the petition blanks and carried them to my desk.
> I felt rather disappointed at the time. The realization dawned upon me that I was a part of a system which was labeled democratic, but was in reality just the opposite. That nominations were given away by benevolent, although autocratic leaders, who could make a public man and who also had the power to unmake him. That the whole system was a sham. (Pp. 118-19)

Again we see Hackenburg's preoccupation with form, with doing things the "right way." The voice of his conscience is loud.

Too loud, apparently, to allow him to remain in politics. A police raid on the party clubhouse in 1926 disclosed that the building was being used as a gambling casino. Shocked by this discovery, Hackenburg began to question his own role. He had served for five years in the New York State Assembly attempting to shut his eyes to the local situation. He explains how feelings of frustration began to oppress him:

> I tried hard to dismiss from my mind the annoying thoughts about the conditions in the district, but they kept returning again and again with a persistence that could not be downed.

I had travelled in a vicious circle. The old political oligarchy, brutal, ignorant and weak, that had misgoverned the neighborhood for a generation, had been smashed to smithereens, mainly through my efforts. I had hoped that the new organization would be representative of the popular will. But the thing was a failure; it had reverted to type. The power had again passed into irresponsible hands; the system was victorious. The realization dawned on me that I had helped to create a Frankenstein, a new idol for the old—whose will was supreme and whose word was law.

I had arrived at the point from which I started; it was the same again as at the beginning. A political machine, once established, continues to function after the reason that brought it into being is gone. The average citizen hates change, is averse to innovation; everything seems to be good enough for him and he wants to leave good enough alone.

I was tired and preoccupied; too discouraged to make another vain effort, single-handed. Moreover, the situation now was different than when, with youthful enthusiasm, we had smashed the useless shell of a weak machine. I knew my limitations and I knew the force and strength of the efficient new local organization. I had helped to build it, I was a part and parcel of it. Yet I felt out of step.

When a boy I spent a summer in an old farmhouse in the country. A few minutes walk from the place there was an abandoned mine that had not been worked for many a decade. It had filled up with water, stagnant, green, ill-smelling. My chums and myself were fascinated with the locality. We used to stand at the brink of the mine and throw stones into the water. On one occasion we discovered a piece of floating driftwood in the center of the pool, and on that piece of lumber a scared, clinging rat. We threw stones at him.

Somehow or other my present situation, melancholy and hopeless, recalled to me this early experience. I had the persistent feeling of being caught in a trap—but, unlike the rat's, my trap was of my own making. (Pp. 289-90)

What is perhaps most striking about Hackenburg's gloomy picture is that it is entirely a subjective one. To the outside world

Hackenburg is doing well, financially and politically. It is only from the viewpoint of his own conscience that he is a trapped rat drowning in stinking water.

In conducting these dialogues with his conscience, Hackenburg's tone of self-reproach is unmistakable. He is not merely angry at the wrongs he sees around him; he condemns himself as partly responsible. In summarizing his mood at the time, Hackenburg stresses his own guilt even more than the wrongdoing of others:

> The entire thing got far beyond me. Morally, I felt responsible, physically I was helpless. I ought to quit. Perhaps it was my duty to quit in protest against a system that was a burlesque of the democratic form of government, a perfect system of taxation without representation.
>
> But I continued my work, consoling myself in the meanwhile with the story of a man who went to a show on a free pass and sat in a good orchestra seat. It was a rotten show, a very bad show. (Pp. 294-95)

Two years later, in 1928, the leaders of Tammany Hall, the New York Democratic organization, invited Hackenburg to perform the ritual reading of the Declaration of Independence at the annual Fourth of July celebration. The invitation was a sign that Hackenburg had moved up in the political world. But he took no pleasure from the distinction:

> Into my doubts and reflections there was constantly injected the disturbing thought that, by keeping silent and by acquiescing in practices that personally I abhorred, I was a part of the bunco game. I tried to get rid of this feeling by telling myself that such was the natural course of things and that no individual was strong enough to change a system. I reassured myself again and again that no one could break through a stone wall by using his head for a ram. But with every repetition this sentiment lost some of its weight. The truth was that my political success was tied up with the system, and my job and the opportunity that it gave me to do the

things I loved to do were the price of my silence. I saw this very clearly and I reproached myself for not having the courage to act. (P. 307)

Hackenburg reports that his moment of decision arrived as he was actually reading the Declaration of Independence to the crowd:

> When my time came to read the Declaration of Independence, I advanced to the center of the platform. My moment of triumph had arrived. I knew the immortal document by heart and started slowly and impressively to recite the Declaration. The words came to me mechanically.
>
> On the outskirts of the crowd, propped up against the walls of the hall, I noticed some men, silent, furtive, quiet. They were reputed to be all powerful; they contributed money to campaign funds, big wads of it, and wielded immense influence because of their financial generosity. No one ever asked where the money came from. It might have been from protected gambling or from padded contracts or from vicious wire-pulling in public offices. They knew the power of the dollar, judicially applied at the psychological moment. They were ready to buy what other men had to sell....
>
> It was ever thus. The royal usurpers were supplanted by the power of the goldbag. A sucker's game. And I was a party to it. Sort of a respectable window dressing—in my small way—covering up the system. A cancer that I had fought in my neighborhood now confronted me on a large scale and I was a proud part of it.
>
> I was bound by party loyalty... nonsense. The real essence of the so-called party regularity is a lurking fear of losing an easy berth and its emoluments, together with all chances of promotion. The loyalty is one of the spine, not of the heart or brains.
>
> The impulse to assert myself and to tear to pieces my connection with all this sham and lie rose overwhelmingly in me.
>
> I finished my reading amid a tense silence. The feeling that filled me I had managed to inject into the recitation. I looked at my audience. Long training in public speaking and knowledge of the

spirit of the crowd convinced me that I had impressed them with an undefined sense of sincerity. I sat down covered with sweat.

After a moment of profound silence a thunder of applause arose in the hall. I paid no attention to it. I knew that I had sung my swan song in Tammany Hall. (Pp. 310-12)

My mind was made up. No matter what the consequences, I would henceforth travel the straight road of duty by myself. (Pp. 314-15)

Hackenburg did quit politics at that time, refusing to run again for his Assembly seat. Later, in 1934, he backed reform mayoral candidate Fiorello La Guardia and was appointed by him a city court judge — a post he held until his death in 1952.

The preceding excerpts vividly illustrate the obligation participant's preoccupation with doing the right thing. In weighing each decision — to enter politics, to continue, to quit — the dictates of conscience are uppermost in Hackenburg's mind.

Hackenburg's perspectives on policy questions reflect the same preoccupation with proper and improper conduct. For Hackenburg, policy issues are not two-sided questions on which reasonable men may disagree. They are issues of right and wrong. Hackenburg reacts to issues on a "gut" level, as simple questions of principle.

One aspect of this dogmatic perspective is the tendency to impugn the motives of opponents, to accuse them of seeking selfish purposes. After all, how else does one explain the holding of the "wrong" position on a clear moral imperative? Throughout his book, Hackenburg attacks the motives and character of those who oppose him. On virtually every issue about which he has a strong conviction — party reform, penal reform, labor reform, public-versus-private power, divorce, blue laws — he portrays his opposition as insincere, selfish, and corrupt. Here, for example, is a brief excerpt of his tirade against the "morals" lobby:

The Blue Sunday brigade, the dry bootleggers auxiliary, the dirty-book-bill busybodies, mass their artillery for a periodic riot of useless propaganda. Their main object is dough; collection for the righteous cause, steady, high salaries, easy living and the sadistic joy that every true blue reformer feels when he is making everybody else in the world unhappy. They get their inane bills introduced by some weak-sister member, break into the newspapers because of the dullness of the session, and return home to collect for the "noble cause." (P. 135)

An obligation type like Hackenburg, then, is extremely subjective, unable to see the other side's point of view. Naturally, this subjectivity leads to contradictions. For example, as a state legislator, Hackenburg fell in with and became a faithful spokesman for the labor lobby in Albany. His admiration for these men expresses the obligation type's characteristic veneration of integrity:

I found real points of contact with these well-informed and determined men. It was a matter of surprise to discover what a well-grounded knowledge of economic causes and effects they possessed.

My previous experience with officials of labor unions had introduced me to a different type of labor politician. In coarseness, in blatant insincerity, in greed and grasp of temporary advantage, most of the labor leaders of my acquaintance were able to give even the average ward politician some fine points.

Here was a group that was different, that was sincere and honest. They renewed my faith in democracy; they offered living proof that intelligent and unselfish leadership could be developed even in materialistic surroundings. (Pp. 162-63)

It never occurs to Hackenburg, as he engages in an eight-page denunciation of lobbyists on the very next pages ("a plague indeed," "awful pests," "rapacious"), that the men he admires fall in the same category.

Occasionally Hackenburg does notice the contradictions into which his absolutist views lead him. But when he does, the revelation does not lead to a broader, more tolerant view. Instead, he feels guilt. We have already seen this response in Hackenburg's reaction to the corruption in the local party organization. While preaching the doctrine of pure politics, Hackenburg finally realized, he was profiting from impure politics. Instead of becoming more tolerant of local party corruption, Hackenburg chose to quit in order to assuage his guilty conscience.

We see the same guilt response in Hackenburg's attitude toward the financial world. After quitting the machine, Hackenburg lost the legal business that the party connection had brought him. He describes how he sought to make up the lost income:

> Until now I had always abhorred real estate speculations; I viewed with horror a system under which fortunes were made out of the prime necessity of shelter. To speculate upon the future development of the community, and to lay a tax on the growth of the city I considered immoral beyond words. The Wall Street Stock Market was to me a cesspool of gambling on a large scale, which I ducked as the devil would the sign of the holy cross.
>
> But I had to find new sources of income, so I went into both, real estate speculation and the stock market. With moderate financial success, and in a conservative way, I engaged in these new activities, embarrassed and mentally disturbed by the fact that in order to uphold the principle of my political decency, I had had to sacrifice my other principles and engage in business activities that were repulsive to my sense of economic fitness. (Pp. 327-28)

For most people, actually participating in real estate and stock market transactions would lead to a degree of tolerance toward these activities. Not for Hackenburg. His experience does not change his view: he just feels guilty.

The sense of inner rightness of obligation types carries over to their perspectives on the policy making process. In their view, policy making ought to be the swift, unfettered enactment of obvious moral principles. Unlike program participants, obligation types have little patience with complex strategies to overcome opposition. For them, opposition to a virtuous cause is wrongful and must be forthrightly exposed and condemned. Unlike the program types, the obligation participants do not value information gathering. Their positions are a priori principles, not judgments reached by investigation and analysis.

In Hackenburg, this intolerant, impatient orientation produced a pyrotechnic legislative style. Finding the Albany legislature unsympathetic to his prescriptions, Hackenburg adopted a disruptive role, scorning opponents, exposing and dramatizing evils, exaggerating. In describing these actions, he makes no claim to superior command of policy issues; he simply believed he was equipped to know truth and others were corrupted.

For example, at the beginning of Hackenburg's first term in the New York state legislature, several measures regulating hydroelectric power were introduced. Hackenburg describes himself as "thoroughly ignorant on the subject" (p. 147). He reports that upon studying the bills, "I could not make head or tail out of them." Nevertheless, he felt — "by instinct," as he puts it — that there was some sinister purpose in the measures (p. 145). He thereupon delivered a "harangue" to the Assembly condemning "mortgaging the wealth of the State to private interests" (p. 149).

Hackenburg frankly describes his disruptive behavior as a member of the New York State Industrial Survey Commission. He had hoped that the commission would propose pro-labor reforms. But the commission contained many members unsympathetic to such measures. It became bogged down in squabbles and was ineffectual in proposing new legislation. That Hackenburg did more than his share to provoke these squabbles is revealed by his own account.

I thought out my position and clearly and deliberately I adopted a very annoying attitude; it took a lot of nerve, but I did it. I questioned everyone's good faith. People hate to be accused of anything. Honest people meet an honest accusation by facing it squarely and readjusting their attitude, if necessary. Dishonest people compromise and run to cover when charges are made against them.

An attempt was made to drag the commission into an investigation of alleged unfair tactics of organized labor. I threw a verbal fit, both at the meeting of the commission and in inspired interviews given out later about the matter. I accused the commission of bad faith. I made a claim that the real purpose of the useless investigation was being made clear. The commission had been created for the purpose of breaking down the slow, painstaking gains of labor. That was a lucky and elegant phrase, and as insulting as anything I could have said. The controversy waxed hot and personal. I became a terrible nuisance, and must have been an awful trial to my unsuspecting colleagues. But the result was accomplished; my threat of an open break over the situation, my public criticism and continuous quibbling had the desired effect. (Pp. 302-3)

The arrogance revealed in this passage is striking. Hackenburg assumes his opponents are "dishonest." He assumes they must respond to his "honest accusation" by "readjusting their attitude"—as if it were impermissible for these opponents to continue to disagree with him. Nor does Hackenburg pause to consider what a legislature would be like where everyone behaved as he did, throwing "verbal fits" and questioning "everyone's good faith." Hackenburg assumes, as the obligation type would assume, that, being right, he is the only one entitled to indignation.

It is not surprising that an obligation type like Hackenburg feels lonely, as if making a one-man crusade against the world. In the first place, obligation types actually do cut themselves off from others by their ostentatious refusal to "play the game" and by impugning the motives of their opponents. But there seems to be another force at work. Obligation types have a need to stand apart, to suffer as an outcast. When one is applauded and successful, there is an uneasiness, a sense of guilt. When one is suffering, reviled by other men for defending a principle, one's conscience glows. There is in the obligation type, then, an impulse toward martyrdom.

The title of Hackenburg's book, *A Solitary Parade,* directly reflects this theme of lonely martyrdom. At many places in the book, Hackenburg reveals the emotional appeal that fighting for lost causes has for him. He describes being outnumbered as exhilarating:

> There were twenty-eight Democrats in the Assembly of 1921 out of a total of one hundred and fifty members, a hopeless minority. I like minorities; in fighting nothing pleases me better than being on the defensive. I have a real flair for infighting. (Pp. 127-28)

Hopeless causes appeal to him:

> During my legislative service on the Capitol Hill I developed the habit of championing lost causes.
>
> The abolition of capital punishment is one of the oldest controversial propositions puzzling and agitating legislative bodies throughout the world. Naturally, I took to it as a duck takes to water and added this cause to the collection of my sincere but vain endeavors.
>
> Determined to stand by, no matter what happened, I continued to introduce my bill to abolish capital punishment at session after session.
>
> I was one in a long line of sincere enthusiasts on the subject, and, like them, I did not get very far with it. Still, I consoled myself with the ennobling thought that I was keeping alive a great and worthy cause. (Pp. 231-32)

Hackenburg takes pleasure in denouncing others even when no policy purpose is served:

Out of the final executive sessions [of the Industrial Survey Commission] there came a compromise measure reducing the legal fifty-four hour week to what amounted to a forty-nine and a half hour week for women in industry. I felt that that ended the controversy; that the world was getting along even without a legislative declaration of changed conditions. Still, I could not deny myself the pleasure of emphasizing my dissent from the quibbling action of a pussy-footing commission. (P. 305)

As Hackenburg's choice of words reveals, being on the outside has a positive emotional appeal for him. The lonely dissent is a "pleasure" he cannot deny himself; he takes to hopeless causes "like a duck to water." Hackenburg wants to be a solitary parade; he wants to go down to defeat in defense of the right.

Other obligation types may not hunger for martyrdom as clearly as Hackenburg does; nevertheless, this theme of seeking lonely, losing struggles is a common obligation perspective. Following the dictates of conscience against the desires of men does create a sense of alienation.

6 The Game Incentive

IN MAKING A LIST of human drives—hunger, sex, status, companionship, and so on—we would rarely be tempted to add a need for competition. Competitive relationships are, of course, a common feature of human activity. But conflict is usually so destructive that it is not easy to believe that human beings positively seek it. We suppose that we aim for harmony and cooperation in our dealings; competition is thought to be an inadvertent and unfortunate by-product. The conviviality participant exhibits what would seem to be the normal orientation: seeking harmonious personal relationships and avoiding conflict.

But there does exist in our makeup a countervailing impulse: to varying degrees, human beings also seek competition. This observation is readily demonstrated by our penchant for sports and games.

While sports and games serve many purposes, the underlying element of these activities is competition. If physical fitness were the only aim, jogging and pushups would suffice. Why have baseball, hockey, football, boxing, handball, water polo, jai-alai, and so on? If only intellectual challenge were sought, certainly scholarship in all its forms and possibilities would fulfill this need. Why have bridge, chess, backgammon, old maid, and monopoly? We appear to have a basic need to compete with each other, to test and demonstrate our skill against other human beings. Struggling with nature is not enough; there is something in us that drives us to struggle with each other.

As with other needs, this drive for competition is unevenly distributed. Some people find competitive games unpleasant and unrewarding. They are joggers by temperament. Others, however, seek out opportunities for competition. They are avid participators in games and sports, zestfully challenging others to match skills against them.

Even though a person may have a strong competitive drive, it does not follow that he will enjoy all games and sports indiscriminately. In addition to the basic ingredient of competition common to all games, each game or sport has peculiar features that make it attractive to one or another type of person. Some games have large elements of luck, others have little or none. Some tax abilities of logic or memory, others do not. Some games suit an energetic temperament, others favor patience. The tennis buff is unlikely to be an avid golfer; the chess devotee is unlikely to be a backgammon enthusiast.

One activity that affords an outlet for those with a strong competitive urge is politics. In politics, one competes with others, employing one's abilities to defeat them in their efforts to gain positions or to enact policies. As with other games, politics has peculiar features: it is inexact, as opposed to logical; it has a large element of luck; it requires working with people; it involves debate and public dispute. Few people would find this combination of features appealing.

But some do. The characteristics of the political game suit their interests and abilities; their strong competitive urge finds a satisfying outlet in political activity. Such participants have a game incentive; they have a need to compete with others in the structured, intellectually challenging interactions that politics affords.

The game participant seeks to demonstrate that he has a better command of a complicated situation, a better grasp of the applicable rules, and better maneuvering skills than his opponents. If he uses his abilities and plays well, he will win: an election, a legislative maneuver, passage of a bill, whatever. His actual enjoyment, however, comes mainly in playing the game. Winning gives the game a point, but the true satisfaction for the game participant lies in demonstrating his ability to play well. His focus is therefore on the tactics, strategies, and manipulations necessary to the winning, rather than on the nature of the victory itself.

The game participant differs in significant ways from other incentive types discussed in this book. Unlike the conviviality type, he is self-confident and active—a doer, not a spectator. Unlike the program type, his focus is on strategies and tactics, not on issues and policy details. He differs markedly from the obligation type in the low emphasis he places on moralistic concerns in politics. In fact, game types characteristically criticize participants who look at the world as it "ought to be" instead of as it "really is."

Finally, the game type differs in a number of ways from the status type. Both types of participants are similar in being rather egocentric, and on this basis alone they might be confused. But in other respects they are different. The status participant focuses on his own personal career, while the game type has a broader view of the entire system. The status type tends to be subjective and partisan in his evaluation of political events and personalities, while the game type is objective and analytical. Finally, the status type tends to be cynical about others and negative toward politics in general, while the game participant respects others and exhibits a zest for the entire realm of politics.

As we have pointed out, each incentive type exhibits a characteristic preoccupation with a particular aspect of political life. For game types, the stress is upon the strategy and tactics of political interaction. It is their favorite theme; it is the subject on which they are most profound and articulate. The general topic of strategy and tactics is not, of course, the exclusive preserve of game types. Practically anyone who discusses politics will find himself analyzing the maneuvers, power positions, and schemes of political participants. Reporters do it; political scientists do it; politicians of all types will do it to some degree. Therefore, the simple existence of a discussion of strategy and tactics in an interview is not sufficient to indicate a game incentive. Game types stress this material more than other participants do; but it occurs, sometimes extensively, in interviews with other types of politicians as well.

What sets the game participant's discussions of strategy and tactics apart from other such discussions is his perspective. The game participant exhibits the orientation of a player in a competitive game. His discussions of strategy and tactics are distinctive in the following ways:

1. He stresses the competitive nature of the interaction.
2. He stresses the excitement and zest of the competition.
3. He is frank in his analysis, laying bare the "real" elements with little regard for appearances.
4. He is objective; he transcends conflicts, viewing himself and opponents as role players.

The first two points perhaps require no explanation. Competition and the zest of competition: these directly reflect the game drive itself. The frankness of the game type stems from his need to reduce politics to its game elements. Politics, as we find it, is diffuse and complicated, laden with the euphemisms, distractions, and rhetoric appropriate to public discourse. It must be reduced to some basic elements in order to be treated as a game. In public, for the playing of the game itself, the game participant will be as long winded and euphemistic as the situation requires. But in his own mind—and for the benefit of a sympathetic listener—the game type is almost ruthlessly frank, stripping politics down to the level of a board game with the moves, positions, and outcomes plainly described.

The objectivity of the politician with a game incentive has two explanations. As a participant who strives to play politics well and successfully, the game type naturally seeks an accurate assessment of the game and its players. Subjectiveness and prejudice would interfere with making this assessment and result in playing the game poorly.

But there is a second explanation of objectivity. The game participant views politics as an activity not engaging his whole being. Although he is a serious and zestful competitor, there is still a part of him not committed to the outcome. He has a peculiar type of dual personality: one part plays the game and the other watches the first part play.

The game type's objectivity should not be misunderstood. One might suppose that participants who treated politics as a "game" would take politics lightly, that they would be unconcerned with victory or defeat. Exactly the reverse is true. Game types are highly committed, energetic participants. The parallel with sports on this point is quite close. We would not say that dedicated athletes are weakly motivated or unconcerned with victory. Look at all the hours of practice, the self-discipline, the fractures and bruises all expended in the cause of defeating the opposition. For the true competitor, winning the game is urgent and it grates on him to be told "it's only a game." The politician with a game incentive has the same orientation. He plays hard and to win. His objectivity is not that of a diffident participant. It is an objectivity revealing his view of politics as a circumscribed contest distinct from "real life."

As we turn to examine two specific politicians with a game incentive, we shall see the importance of these points. We shall be looking not merely at discussions of strategy and tactics, but at the game type's peculiar stress on competition, frankness, and objectivity.

I. Gordon Hart: "I'm Competitive and Love This Kind of Thing"

Gordon Hart is a councilman in the Maine town of Newbury.* He is fifty years old, a Democrat. After retiring from a business career in New York, he returned to his boyhood town with the definite intention of going into politics. He studied political science in college and teaches an occasional course in practical politics at the local high school.

In the interview with him, we find him repeatedly dwelling on the subject of strategy and tactics. Indeed, the interview is virtually an extended discussion of political calculations and maneuvers, broken only by perfunctory answers to the interviewer's questions on other subjects. Early in the interview, Hart begins to detail the strategy he followed to work his way into the local political scene: becoming active in clubs, writing letters to the newspapers, making what he calls "tentative probes." He continues to recount how the first definite act to recruit him took place:

> HART: I'll tell you how [my first nomination] came about. I had been to the Democratic caucus to see how it operated and to watch the people and to have a slight voice in the feeling of who makes the decisions at this kind of thing and there was a man who was going to run, the Democrat who had run [and lost two years before], and he's not a very attractive candidate. About four weeks later, there was a public meeting where the School Board and the Town Council were quarreling over the proposed budget in the town, and the Town Council had recommended a very large cut, some seven-

---

*The name and town of this respondent have been changed to protect his identity.

ty or eighty thousand dollars from the school budget, and the preschoolers were up in arms. There was a large public meeting—some two hundred or so people, which is a large crowd for Newbury—and feelings were running high. Everyone was given a chance to speak, and I made an impassioned three-minute, well-phrased argument *for* the school people. That happens to be my bias, and Joe Bass [local Democratic chairman], who was at the meeting, when I sat down said, "Why the hell don't you run for the legislature? You're getting a big fat government paycheck every month. Do something for your country." That's just what I wanted to hear. (laughs) I said, "I'll do it!"

In this passage we notice, first, the delight that Hart takes in manipulating people and situations. We also see how he turns a political interaction into a game with preplanned moves and clever ploys. He didn't just happen to make a speech that impressed Joe Bass; he sees himself skillfully contriving this outcome. Hart's candidness is also striking. He is frankly and unabashedly proud of his calculating strategy. There is no disposition—which a status type would exhibit—to hide the unflattering elements of deviousness and egocentrism in the episode.

We notice, lastly, the objective tone this account displays. In reporting the school controversy, Hart is neutral. Even though he took sides, he is unconcerned with the "real" merits of the issue. He calls his own preference a "bias"—which is exactly how a neutral observer would describe it.

Later in the interview, Hart is asked about the council meetings. He agrees with the interviewer that they are mostly rather dull. Then he is asked if there are more exciting parts:

Q: Are there any parts of the meeting that are not boring?
HART: Oh yes. When there is a chance to educate the council into something that is relatively important, little things such as... or when a challenge develops. It appears that my Republican opponent for the legislature this fall is another council member. And it appears that the challenge has been arising, and he also is the very

conservative faction of the council. When I detect a challenge or a difference of opinion arising from him, I love this kind of thing.

Q: What happens is you have a debate right there?

HART: Yes, open debate right there.... I express my philosophy, he expresses his, I try and cast a little aspersion, a little shadow on his, he does it to me. Then we maneuver for the vote. And I consistently have won these little skirmishes that have come up over relatively unimportant things.

We see in this excerpt the primacy of competition for the game type. Hart begins by pointing vaguely to the activity of "educating the council" and then trails off to rush into the point that really attracts him—challenge. This theme of competition continues on for over three pages (see below). He turns debating into a competitive game. His frankness is almost breathtaking; he strips the interaction down to what he feels is the basic element—a duel in which the object is to make the other guy look bad. The rest of us believe that debate serves functions of expressing ideals, swaying the public, and making policy on a reasonable basis. Hart ignores these aspects—and our sensibilities—to get at what he feels is the heart of the game.

It is evident from this passage that Hart does not dislike his opponent. He views him objectively, as a role-player who gives as good as he gets. This respect for opponents is a deeply rooted characteristic of the game type. A game type requires worthy opponents; without them there would be no challenge, for only worthy opponents can provide the desired competitive encounters. For all other types of participants, opponents are an unavoidable nuisance—or worse; political life would be more pleasant or more constructive if opponents would disappear. For the game participant, however, opponents are central to the satisfaction he seeks.

The continuation of the preceding excerpt is worth reporting in its entirety as a classic game discussion of strategy and tactics:

Q: Well, how do you maneuver when there are so few people [seven on the council]? What is your strategy?

HART: Well, I have to figure how each man is going to vote and to whom you are going to appeal. Now the issue comes up that we are going to talk about — the dogcatcher — and I know how one man will vote. And I predict in advance, and I know damn well his vote. And I know there's another man who generally likes me and will go along on most issues with me... so here are three votes. I just need one more man, and I analyze the four people, less the one against whom I'm competing, and I see which man I think might be a likely sales prospect. Then I figure what angle would appeal to him of this question, and then I aim it at him. Although I don't aim it at him deliberately. I do it by means of debate or roundabout questions or let the thing occur to him indirectly, and then I call for a vote.

Q: You do this... while the iron is hot, you don't think it about it beforehand? It is sort of as is?

HART: That's right. As a rule you don't know that anything is going to be an issue beforehand. This is a very rare thing. You see the agenda come up for the night and you don't realize it is going to be a major issue. I'll give you a good little example. We have in Newbury a system of voting on a ticket that you punch. What it is is an IBM card really — when you pull it out it goes right to the IBM machine. And it's a poor system. It cost me, I know, thirty-four invalidated votes in 1970 and I just lost by a little more than one hundred, so it begins to count, and it hurts my Jeffersonianism. There are some of the old folks who don't like it — they don't see very well and they are ashamed to say it and they don't understand the system, and it is tiny and you have to punch — well, I don't want the damned thing. I think we should go back to paper ballots.

So the issue came up to the council two or three meetings ago. We're going to have a March election, and we shall authorize the election, you have to authorize it by law, you know, you have a warden and all this jazz, and what kind of ballot he shall use, and of course the town clerk asks for this card thing. He likes it and it's easy and all that. So before the council meeting, I called three other men and said, "Hey, how do you feel about this computer ballot? I'm dead set against this." And two said, "Yeah, hate the damned thing, sure, whatever you want." And the other one said, "Oh, I don't know anything about it, whatever you want, Gordon."

And I said, well that's my four votes and I'll go in and keep my mouth shut. And when the issue arises, I'll just move for the paper ballots, that he be instructed. And then I did move, whereupon one of the other councillors called upon the town clerk to ask him what he thought. And the town clerk gave an impassioned defense on how great these ballots were and how they saved money and how the error had been steadily declining in the last five elections and it was now down to infinitesimal, and it was so much more efficient, it was modern, and all the other towns were going to it, and our town ought to be modern, too.

And my man in the middle who had said, "Yeah, I'd do whatever you want Gordon, I don't know much about it," I could see him begin to defect. "Oh well," he says, "I didn't know all that," et cetera, et cetera. And then the problem became, how can I, in the short debate time that we will have, in the next ten or fifteen minutes, I've got to find somebody, some fourth vote. I'm going to lose him. It's obvious that the plea for modernity and efficiency has swayed him, and I'm going to lose him.

There is one other man there who is very conservative, down-to-earth, put a dollar in the bank every week to buy a new car in three years, that kind of thing. So I changed my whole pitch. I said, "This is the basic right," and I gave an impassioned speech — the idea was that if we disenfranchised one elder citizen then we've failed our damn trust — and I got his vote! (laughs) But there were practically no other grounds on which I could have appealed to that man. In other words, it's an individual analysis of the man from whom we need the vote.

In this excerpt, Hart exhibits the game characteristics noted thus far. He stresses the competitive nature of the episode. The actual merits of the issue are not his primary concern. He lacks the program type's keen interest in the substance of policy. He says only a few words about why he prefers paper ballots; the rest of the excerpt dwells on the calculations and manipulations of the contest. He frankly reduces the episode into a contest of coalition building, treating reason and arguments as mere ploys in the game. His objectivity extends to calling his own argument on the right to a paper ballot a "pitch." He harbors no animosity toward his opponent, the city clerk who broke down his original coalition. To the contrary, he respects him as a worthy opponent who provided an exciting test of skill.

Another trait of the game type is self-confidence. Throughout the interview, Hart is frank in reporting his abilities and cleverness. In this respect, game participants are the opposite of conviviality types, who avoid the appearance of bragging. In announcing his abilities, however, the game type is not attempting to compensate for some insecurity. He is simply revealing his frank, self-confident orientation. He has nothing to hide; he just as readily will assess his own faults:

> Q: Could you give some sort of overview of your strengths and weaknesses in campaigning? Have you learned certain things that you can do better than others?
>
> HART: Yes. I come on very quickly. I come on strongly, and I come on quickly and I communicate very well with others and I have an empathy for how people are feeling. And I can talk to people quickly, readily, and easily, and I impress them because I am very verbal, as you can see. And when I'm under pressure and my adrenalin is running, I can form little *bon mots* very quickly, and this I would class as probably my chief strength in a person-to-person debate, particularly where there is a little excitement involved. I am almost masterful, and this is a strength, may you understand.
>
> Q: Do you have any weaknesses that hurt you?
>
> HART: Yuh, I'm very emotional, and you can get to me every now and then. And if there is anything a politician shouldn't show when he's in debate, you shouldn't be able to get to him. Now Ed

Muskie's got a temper when he's debating with Nixon. He should be wiser and be able to set him aside, you know, this kind of thing. And I'm a little weak there. You can get to me and you get some "God damn's" out of me in open debate. And I tend to make too broad a statement at times, and people suspect me. And, finally, when I'm in a hurry and I have a long complicated thought to get across, I will attempt to reduce it to some kind of small analogy or a quick description which people without my — let's face it — educational or communicative background may not grasp or if they do grasp, they feel I'm putting a cheap shot in, if you know what I mean. So I'm working very hard on that, on the low-key kind of thing.

In several other places in the interview, we see Hart's willingness to recognize his faults and make efforts to overcome them. He discusses his first race, for state representative, in these terms. Hart knowingly entered the contest as a "sacrificial lamb" in order to get experience and exposure.

Q: What did you get from the whole overall experience?

HART: Oh, how to communicate with people; that's the important thing! Who has to be reached and how you reach them, and the kind of issues they'll listen to and what they hear when you speak to them. Oh my goodness, as good as I am in that kind of thing, my eyes were opened. It did one other valuable thing for me, too. I became drunk on my own excitement. As I say, I'm competitive and love this kind of thing and by November — at some point, along about the latter part of September or early part of October — I had allowed myself to become totally hypnotized and believe that I might win. And this taught me a valuable lesson on that at four thirty in the morning on the third of November (laughs): to go back to my old cynical self and appraise things from a poker point of view, not get too excited simply because you have a few good cards in your hand. So, I learned not to become too overenthusiastic, and I learned a great deal about the skills of communicating, who needs to be talked to, how you talk to them.

Hart criticizes himself for self-deception. He got so carried away by the campaign that he could no longer assess his own chances objectively. The game type's ability to step back and note his own shortcomings is unusual among political participants.

We see in this excerpt another game characteristic, the tendency to employ analogies from sports and games. However, one must not place too much weight on this point in determining incentives from interviews. Other types of participants will also, on occasion, employ sports analogies. One of the most common mistakes the beginning coder makes is to see a sports analogy or the word "game" in an interview and, disregarding everything else, advance a game-incentive classification for the subject. (On pages 114-15, for example, we find Frederick L. Hackenburg, a clear obligation type, using the word "game.")

In their analyses of political strategy, game types are comprehensive and well organized—a natural consequence of the attention they devote to this subject. They enjoy, for example, advancing lists of factors that bear on a tactical situation. Here is Hart explaining why he will win the legislative seat he failed to gain two years earlier:

> HART: For one thing, this is a presidential election, and there's going to be a large number of voters come out; somewhere in excess of twenty-five hundred people will be out.... As you know, the increased vote tends by and large to be Democratic. Two, I've been very visible for the last year: Town Council, hard working, chief fund raiser for the church, active Lion, and all this jazz. Too, there's not been a phone call, there's not been a person that's wanted something that hasn't heard from me. I go and make an appointment. Then, three, the incumbent is no longer running. He's retired, and a new candidate will arise. And the present man who has the nomination papers out for the Republicans is not as strong a candidate as the last one. And I'm going to work like hell!

A concise diagnosis like this is not produced off the cuff. Clearly Hart has been working the subject over in his mind for some time.

Game types are also extremely sensitive to the requirements of role playing. Politics is a complex set of interrelationships. The same individual has to play different roles as circumstances change. And each political position has a set of role expectations attached to it, which the holder must fulfill to be successful. The game participant understands that you adjust your behavior to conform to your current role. Hart illustrates this perspective in the following exchange:

> Q: As a liberal from a small town, would you be able to operate with the larger-city machine Democrats?
> HART: Oh yes, sure. I would have no qualms whatsoever about operating with them. How I would operate in Augusta and how I would talk about it with the folks in Newbury are two separate things. Because I would vote organizationally with the party except in the most dire of circumstances. I firmly believe in the party discipline, but I won't say that in Newbury. [In Newbury I say] "I vote for the issue." You've got to. I don't mind that.

In the above excerpt, Hart sees two roles: state legislator and local campaigner. He has no difficulty adjusting to their opposite demands. As a state legislator, he votes with his party; as a local campaigner, he stresses his independence of party.

The game type's orientation toward the objective analysis of political interaction leads to another feature frequently encountered in game interviews: the enunciation of rules for successful interaction. The game participant is almost like a coach, passing along practical tips, the do's and don't's of everyday politics. We find Hart making many such statements:

> You have to be very careful about asking people [for their opinion] because you'll get a few people who talk so damn much and so vehemently that they tend to sway you. It's always the same guy, so you have to learn to weigh their opinions.

Who was it that said that "If a man would gain and hold power, he must learn to suffer fools gladly"? I can sit there for two hours.

I have never really stuck it to anyone. The job of the party leader is to get votes. If you truly cut someone up, there's one vote you can never again count on for anything.

If you're willing to work hard and you're efficient, you can get a lot done in a short time, which I can. I think this will come to your advantage, if you're willing to help someone else, and if you abstain entirely from personal attacks or from vendettas, and you keep your mouth shut until you find out who speaks and means what they say — all of these basic things of getting along in life.

You don't attack a man directly. Perfectly all right to disagree with him, but you don't impugn his motives or his intelligence or his honesty or anything of that nature.

In this line of work, promises are absolutely vital. Your personal word becomes your bond. It's about the only currency a politician has to work with.

Two of the rules that Hart gives — don't get personal and keep your word — are especially important for game types. They want to keep politics a wholesome, circumscribed activity. Therefore, they view personal attacks as bad sportsmanship, which threaten the limited character of the game. Keeping one's word is important for injecting an element of predictability into politics. If players won't keep agreements, then coalition building and compromises are difficult to arrange. The game type is especially sensitive to the importance of keeping his word. He realizes that his trustworthiness marks him as a player to be reckoned with — as a professional, not a flighty amateur.

Even when discussing his own experiences, the game participant often passes along general pointers:

HART: Incidentally, this again is the kind of thing that's important in a small town: I was very, very careful in my fall campaign never to bad-mouth my opponent. I don't believe at any time or to anybody outside perhaps the bosom of my family, did I ever indicate by so much as a hesitation or a wink that I had any fault whatsoever to find with my opponent, who was a seventy-three-year-old man, a great, impeccable person, who has been a lifetime friend of old citizens.... In a small town, this gets back, so this was reflecting to my advantage: "Well, Hart was pretty nice when he ran against old Eben, and I'll vote for him for the Council" kind of thing.

In explaining his strategy for victory, Hart reveals a general rule that guided him: don't attack highly esteemed figures in a small town.

Another rule stressed by the game type is the need to restrain egotism in the interest of collective purposes. In a game that pits one team against another, you have no chance of winning if you don't cooperate with your own team. In fact, without cohesive groups, you don't have a game anymore. Here is Hart explaining why he is a strong believer in parties:

> HART: How the hell is the system going to function without parties? How are you going to state policy? I tell the students all the time, I say it about twice a week: "Twenty-two people on the field, you can't have a football game until you choose up sides and decide what kind of a game you're going to play instead of just running around."

Politicians who break group norms for egocentric purposes destroy the game itself:

> It's a pain in the neck. If you try to have a ski team, and you have somebody who has not learned the rules of skiing, or if you have a basketball team, and the man insists on playing with a baseball, then it reduces the efficiency and the pleasure of the operation. It is frustrating and difficult.

A game where participants do not play together and play fair ceases to be enjoyable. The pleasure of engaging in calculations and competition is lost. For the game participant, then, working as a team and playing by the rules are basic precepts.

Game participants enjoy politics. We have seen this zest exhibited throughout the Hart interview. When asked directly about satisfactions, Hart is unhesitating:

> Q: In you overall view of campaigns, do you find these enjoyable?
> HART: Very, very. I'd like to work eighteen hours a day; the adrenalin runs all the time. I love to hear the phone ring.

In their enjoyment of politics, game types are clearly distinguished from status and obligation types, who are rather negative about politics. Conviviality and program types usually enjoy politics and view it positively, but rarely with the unrestrained enthusiasm of the game participants.

As an outgrowth of their positive attitude, game types are quite pleased to call themselves "politicians." Hart, for example, says, "I'm proud to be a politician; they [other councilmen] consider it a dirty word." One cannot help feeling, in hearing game types embrace politics, that they are making an objective as well as a subjective point. All the other incentive types seem somewhat misfitted for politics, carrying on in their peculiar ways in opposition to the nature of the enterprise. Game types seem to have found their métier in politics. It is almost as if the activity had been invented especially for them.

It is instructive to examine Hart's future plans. In the interview, he forthrightly announces his intention to run for the state legislature and assesses his chances as "from good to unbeatable." The drive for upward mobility in a game type like Hart stems not from a status-seeking impulse. Game types want to move to a higher level because the stakes and the challenges are greater. Again, the parallel with sports is quite close. The serious competitor feels a pressure to move to the "big leagues" to test his abilities against better players.

The impulse of game types to compete at higher levels means that few game types will be encountered at the small-town, local level. Hart, as a small-town councilman, is an exception. However, since he subsequently did win the legislative seat, he is an exception that proves the rule.

II. CHARLES B. LIPSEN: "I WANTED TO BE AT THE CENTER OF THE ACTION"

Charles Lipsen, our second example of a game participant, has spent most of his adult life in Washington politics. He came to the capital in the late 1940s. Since then, he has held numerous political jobs, including congressional aide, campaign manager, and presidential assistant. His major occupation, however, has been that of lobbyist. At one time or another, he represented the direct-mail industry, dairymen in their fight against oleomargarine producers, the Retail Clerks International Union, and the National Cable Television Association.

Lipsen describes his experiences and perspectives in an autobiographical work entitled *Vested Interest*.[1] As with the other autobiographies we have discussed, this book is a loosely structured, personal account of the author's life in politics. Strict chronology is not adhered to. Exact dates of key events are often difficult to ascertain. It contains no notes or references, not even a table of contents. The work is a frank, personally focused account of the type appropriate for incentive analysis.

Lipsen sees himself as a man naturally suited to politics, and suited, more specifically, to the phases of politics involving manipulation and interaction. "Officially," he says, "I became a lobbyist on April 23, 1957.... In reality, I think I've been a lobbyist all my life" (p. 19).

He traces his political orientation back to his experience in the Marines during World War II, choosing, significantly, a sports illustration:

> In fact, I learned a lot about lobbying from my years in the Marines.

I learned my first lesson before going to the front lines, however. At 147 pounds, I was boxing champ of my company and had won more than twenty fights in my weight class when I was matched against a marine named Tommie Tomlinson from Michigan. I was confident of victory—until twelve seconds into the first round, when Tomlinson broke my nose. Later, he tinned my ear. My only success was in landing a few jabs and managing to stay on my feet throughout the three-round fight. I learned from that experience to get to know my opposition before getting into a fight. I hadn't known, for example, that Tommie Tomlinson had been a Golden Glove finalist. (Pp. 20-21)

After the war, Lipsen's aspiration was to be an FBI agent, but exposure to local politics in Wisconsin changed that:

A new bug had bitten me there and then. No longer did I crave the FBI. Washington was, as young people came to say, where it was at. And, true to form, I wanted to be at the center of the action. (P. 32)

Consistent with our theory that the game type heads for the big leagues, Lipsen has spent his entire adult life in Washington politics. Once out of law school, he packed his bags and headed to the capital. He apparently gave no thought to remaining in Wisconsin for a try at state or local government. Like other game types, he wanted to be "at the center of the action."

Later, after several years as congressional aide and lobbyist, Lipsen reports:

I was growing to love politics. It had all the glamor and excitement of war—its strategy, its intelligence gathering, its plots to outwit the opposing force—without its concomitant bloodshed. (P. 70)

Lipsen's hunger for competitive involvement is perhaps best illustrated by his reaction to being deprived of that involvement. In 1969 he left active lobbying to work in a Washington law firm, where he dealt mainly with arranging government contracts. Financially he was highly successful, but he found life away from politics a purgatory:

....I often found that I could make my calls and contacts for my clients in little more than half a day. I started hitting the hangouts to see old friends. Some would join me for a quick drink and then hustle back to work. But while they each had one drink with me, I had at least one with each of the half-dozen people I might run into. I was putting on pounds, and I was afraid I was becoming an alcoholic.

So I started going home in the afternoons, instead. I'd flip on the television and watch "As the World Turns," "The Edge of Night," and an occasional afternoon movie. But I found myself hitting the liquor cabinet as well. While I watched the daily travails of characters in the soap operas, I was slugging down at least a pint of scotch.

[My wife] Janice, meanwhile, had gone to work in the office of Speaker of the House Carl Albert. By the time she got home, I was in my cups, too tired to go out, and our social and personal life started dwindling to nothing.

For the first time in my life, I was making real money. And instead of enjoying it, I was boozing it away—along with ignoring my wife and family. I was risking my health and happiness at the very time I should have been enjoying the new security.

Perhaps I was too immature to handle a sudden spurt of income. Perhaps I was wrong never to have developed a hobby like woodworking. Whatever the reason, it couldn't go on. I was getting too much for doing too little. It should have been fun, but I missed the action of tramping the hallways of Congress. And I was becoming a lush....

So when I heard that the National Cable Television Association was hunting for a chief lobbyist, I lunged at it.... (Pp. 173-75)

This excerpt vividly illustrates the compulsive nature of an incentive. Lipsen had what we normally suppose is the ideal situation: too much pay for too little work. Yet he was unhappy. An emotional need drove him back to politics; he missed the challenge, the competition, the action.

Lipsen's choice of title for the book, *Vested Interest*, suggests his incentive. Instead of being hesitant and apologetic about being a lobbyist, Lipsen is forthrightly proud of his job. On page one, Lipsen's first anecdote has him frankly introducing himself as "a lobbyist" to President Ford. The last anecdote of the book makes the same point:

> In 1965, not long after Hubert Humphrey had been inaugurated as Vice-President, he made a speech at the twenty-fifth convention of the Retail Clerks. In his remarks, he said:
> "By the way, I was met at the door by my friend Chuck Lipsen. Chuck is about the best—I won't say 'lobbyist' because that isn't what he is—but adviser and counselor to the Congress of the United States. He does a great job."
> That was nice to hear, especially from the Vice-President of the United States. But Hubert was wrong. I *am* a lobbyist.
> I like what I do. (Pp. 183-84)

Humphrey, sensitive to the niceties of image in politics, avoids the somewhat derogatory term "lobbyist"; but Lipsen embraces it. Here we see the game type's impulse to strip away euphemism and call the players by their "real" names.

The principal theme of *Vested Interest* is political tactics and strategy, the main preoccupation of the game participant. Indeed, aside from the few pages on his boyhood and early years, Lipsen dwells on this topic almost exclusively. His many anecdotes usually show him as the main actor in complex situations, maneuvering successfully in competition with others. Through these incidents, he points out the rules for successful political action.

In a typical example of this focus on strategy and tactics, Lipsen tells about the time he was simultaneously supporting the campaigns of Hale Boggs for Majority Leader in the House and Hugh Scott for Minority Leader in the Senate:

> They were campaigns that had to be pushed in differing manners. Boggs was opposed by, among others, Morris Udall, a bril-

liantly effective liberal congressman from Arizona. But Boggs was an old friend and, though further to the right than Udall, a man who was closer to the middle of the political spectrum in his party and therefore, in my opinion, then better able to develop party unity. Scott, meanwhile, was opposed by Roman Hruska of Nebraska and Howard Baker of Tennessee. Of the three, Scott was considered by far the most friendly to labor and social causes.

So on the one hand, I was pushing Boggs because of his moderation and, on the other, helping Scott because of his relative liberalism. So to the Republicans in the Senate, my pitch was to avoid naming a "Neanderthal" as leader (which was an unfair but effective characterization of Scott's opponents), and to the Democrats in the House it was to steer clear of naming a "knee-jerk liberal."...

One of the most effective methods I used was to establish — by word of mouth — that both Scott and Boggs were the odds-on favorites for their respective leadership jobs. A couple of carefully planted news items, identifying some key members who were quietly working for my candidates, strengthened that notion. Then I would call on the members and tell them, in effect, they had better get on the bandwagon. If they did, they could count on patronage assistance — good committee assignments for themselves and support for local projects that would help get them votes in their next campaigns. If they didn't, I suggested facetiously, good government might dictate that others, not them, would get the plums dispensed by the leaders. (Pp. 176-77)

In this excerpt, we note several of the key game characteristics. Lipsen strives for an objective analysis of the situation. He can stand back and analyze his own actions dispassionately, even pointing to their demagogic aspect (his "pitch" was to name opponents "Neanderthals" or "knee-jerk liberals"). He stresses his own role as main actor in the circumstances ("I was pushing"; "I suggested"; "I used"). He brings to his role a certain good humor ("I suggested facetiously"). And finally, he passes along pointers: support moderates; create the impression that your candidate is sure to win; hint at future favors in return for present support.

Lipsen's account of how he became close to Lyndon Johnson further illustrates his preoccupation with strategy and tactics. He says: "I didn't just happen into [Johnson's] confidence" (p. 112). He "worked diligently" to do favors for Johnson while he was still Senate Majority Leader. In one incident, Johnson had promised Lipsen he would support a key labor bill. Later, Johnson decided the bill was too liberal for his constituency and asked Lipsen if he could renege.

"Can I get off the hook on the minimum wage bill?" [Johnson] asked, peering down at me.

Obviously, I was troubled. Johnson support would almost guarantee Senate passage. Without it, it would be a toss-up. On the other hand, this man was too powerful a legislator to cross. Sure, I knew he'd stick with me if I insisted on it by telling him how much I had been counting on him and that I had already told other senators and other lobbyists of his position. A change would mean going back to everyone I had induced into supporting us on the basis that the majority leader was in our corner. But if I held him to it, I was afraid it might be the last favor he'd ever do for me.

"Leader," I said, "give me a day. If I can pick up a couple of votes that are marginal right now, you're off."

He thanked me and I left. The other votes really didn't matter. We'd get them or we wouldn't. But I wanted Johnson to think I would have a lot of extra work to do because of his decision to renege. That way he'd remember I had done a favor for *him*. (P. 115)

We can see the wheels turning in Lipsen's head as he debates the pros and cons of letting Johnson back off from his pledge. Finally, he hits on the ideal device, one that involves a short-term setback but insures a long-term relationship with a powerful ally. Lipsen clearly enjoys recounting this tactical problem and the successful way he handled it.

At times, Lipsen leaves his anecdotes to describe his general strategy for achieving power in Washington politics. These passages especially suggest a game incentive. As we have already stressed, a participant's motivation is revealed by the subjects on which he concentrates. The subject to which Lipsen returns time and again is the technique of influencing people and wielding power. In the following passage, Lipsen explains one of his tactics:

> Most lobbyists arrange their vacations to coincide with congressional recesses, when the members leave Washington and go home for a week or a month. Not me. When Congress goes home, most of the staff members stay behind and continue working to prepare projects that must be ready when the members return. But at least they have more time to spare than they do when a session is in progress. So I use that time to drop around to different offices and take staff people out to lunch. At first, most of them are surprised I would even bother. Then they are astounded to learn I have nothing up my sleeve that I'd like presented to the congressman when he gets back to Washington. Those lunches have paid off tenfold in my ability to get through to a congressman I need to reach no matter how busy the man may be. Having key staff people as your friends is often more important than golfing once a month with the majority leader.
>
> It was through the simple but time-consuming expedient of seeing as many people as possible as often as possible that I was able to achieve that most precious commodity of lobbying—access. Some lobbyists could get it with endless supplies of money. Some could get it because they were personages (like former senators or high-level aides to a former President) in their own right. I had neither enormous financial resources nor was I then or now an "important" person in Washington.
>
> But in time it enabled me to win important victories from the disparate likes of John Kennedy, Lyndon Johnson—and even that symbol of rock-hard conservatism himself, Barry Goldwater. (P. 111)

We notice that Lipsen's ultimate aim is "to win important victories." Techniques and strategies are devised to fit this end. Significantly, the sentence stressing "victories" closes out this chapter entitled "The ABC's of Lobbying."

Lipsen sees himself as a competitor. He describes a running battle he had with a fellow labor lobbyist, Andrew Biemiller. Biemiller thought labor should support only its staunchest congressional adherents. Lipsen argued that labor should also back more marginal supporters, in hopes of getting their occasional vote on some issues. Of Biemiller's viewpoint, he says:

> To be sure, his philosophy was clearly purer than my own. But, in the long run, mine won more battles in the halls of Congress if fewer on the editorial pages. (P. 101)

We note here the game type's stress on influence and winning battles rather than on the prestige of editorial page recognition.

Lipsen goes on to recount a minor victory he scored over Biemiller. Proceeding, in his usual fashion, to touch base with congressmen not automatically considered friendly to labor, he discovered an unexpected supporter in the new senator from Texas, Lloyd Bentsen. He gloats:

> In finding that the new Texas senator was, in fact, a potentially strong ally of labor, I had scored a lobbying coup that I was determined to milk to its limit. (P. 103)

Lipsen used this information to embarrass Biemiller at a meeting of all Washington labor lobbyists. Lipsen describes Biemiller's reaction:

> Biemiller glared at me. He knew I had sprung the news on him in this manner to make the greatest possible impression on the other lobbyists. It was a point for my side in our running battle over which congressmen to court and, more importantly, which to spend labor's political money on when it came to election time.

But he was too smart—and too gentlemanly—to challenge in front of the others what I knew he believed to be questionable information. Many in the group were newer at the game than either of us. At the least, he did not want to discourage dissent by openly embarrassing me. (P. 104)

We see here Lipsen's competitive instincts coming to the fore. We also see another game trait—the respect for worthy opponents. Biemiller is "smart" and "gentlemanly."

In another passage, we see Lipsen's regard for a capable adversary. He was fighting Nixon's nomination of G. Harrold Carswell to the Supreme Court. His main opponent was the White House lobbyist, Ken Belieu. Lipsen presents Carswell's rejection by the Senate as largely his own doing. He persuaded key senators at the last minute to vote against Carswell. After his victory, he discusses his competitor:

Ken was a pro, all right, but he had made his own tactical mistake. He had gotten commitments, all right, but not from the members themselves. He had spoken to their staff people....

Soon, it was over and we had won. Later in the afternoon, while we were back at the union offices celebrating, I got a phone call. It was Ken Belieu.

"It's always tough to lose a big one," Ken said, "but I wanted to congratulate you. You did a helluva job and you whipped us fair and square."

"You're some kind of guy," I said, genuinely touched. "Listen, I didn't mean to be a smart-ass yesterday."

"Hell, don't worry about that," he said. "It just showed me I had counted wrong. You're just damned lucky I wasn't able to pull those people back away from you. It would have been a different ball game."

It was a couple of weeks later that I learned Ken had called me only minutes after having been reprimanded by H. R. Haldeman in the presence of the President, even though Belieu had not predicted victory—only a close vote. To congratulate his opponent after having been dressed down in front of the President took more than a good loser. It took a good man. (Pp. 168-69)

Like Gordon Hart, Lipsen enjoys passing along the dos and don'ts of politics—the practical rules for successful interaction. He wants to go beyond his own experience to generalize about the political process itself. Here are a few tips culled from *Vested Interest:*

> Courting staff members is a basic to successful lobbying. (P. 64)
>
> Meeting [congressman] takes shoe-leather and patience. Winning them over, however, requires more; it takes proving your reliability and dependability. (P. 6)
>
> [P]olitics... requires taking care of those who toiled in your vineyard, even through a drought. (P. 98)
>
> You can't count on people from your own party or even your regular friends to support you all the time. It's important to touch base with everybody, even those you don't expect you'll pick up. (P. 69)
>
> [T]he best way to reach politicians on the issues is by giving them money for campaigns, doing personal favors, and providing free manpower to help their re-election. (P. 6)

The game type prides himself on being a political analyst; he enjoys offering his insights to others.

This ability to analyze politics extends to himself. The game type can stand back from an event and dispassionately discuss his own role in it—even his own shortcomings. The Carswell anecdote illustrates this point. Lipsen tells the correct actions he took to achieve his end: he spoke directly to the key, undecided senators just before the vote; he presented telling arguments simply and clearly; and so on. Proud of his ability to sway the result, he criticizes his main rival, Ken Belieu, for a tactical error: getting commitments from staff aides only, not from the senators themselves. But then Lipsen admits a major error of his own. In his elation at finding the votes to defeat Carswell, he boasts to Belieu about the senators pledged to him. Later, he criticizes himself for allowing emotion to overcome good judgment:

> In my eagerness to flaunt my victory over the opposition, to make sure that the other side knew that I, Charles Lipsen, had been responsible for pulling the key uncommitted votes to my side, I had been guilty of the worst kind of strategic error. It was no different from telling an opposing general in a war where, when and in what numbers your troops planned to launch a devastating attack. (P. 167)

This ability to see himself objectively brings the game type self-knowledge that might be useful in future political maneuvers.

Another trait of the game participant is pragmatism. Lipsen is not out to change the world. Instead, he accepts people and their goals as he finds them. Commenting on a senator's dalliance with a call girl, he says:

> I was hardly anyone to make judgments about the morals of others. Besides, I figured that I didn't care whether a senator liked to play cribbage or not. Why should I care if he liked to play house? (P. 9)

This matter-of-fact approach allows the game type to interact harmoniously with every kind of politician. Lipsen has cooperated with such varied political figures as Barry Goldwater, Strom Thurmond, Margaret Chase Smith, Hugh Scott, Lloyd Bentsen, George Meany, Lyndon Johnson, and Hubert Humphrey. He describes his practical aim in these contacts:

> I learned early both the ease with which a Democrat could work with a Republican and, more important, the necessity of doing so if one was to be a successful lobbyist. (P. 69)

Lipsen's pragmatic nature is coupled with two other characteristics typical of the game participant: a low sense of moral outrage and a lack of ideological fervor. Indeed, Lipsen complains more than once about "moral purists." They don't understand how politics works (p. 6), and their purism constitutes "a danger to politics in America" (p. 57). His opposition to rigidity stems from a wish to keep options open and to avoid alienating potential allies. He approvingly quotes advice given him by Sam Rayburn:

> "Never... cut anybody off from contact, even if you think your philosophies are like night and day. This year's enemy may turn out to be your strongest ally next year. Times change, constituencies change and members change on issues." (P. 114)

The game type's pragmatism extends to easy acceptance of whatever political practices happen to be prevailing. For instance, Lipsen has no trouble accepting, even defending, the patronage system — even after its implementation cost him a job when Republicans took over Congress in 1952:

> That was patronage and, while it cost me my job, I couldn't complain about it. It was part of how the spoils system worked. If you backed the right horse, you won your bet. If you supported the right candidate, there was gold at the end of that rainbow, too. (P. 38)

His adaptability even allows him to accept the rules of the game in a nondemocratic country, when these suit his purposes. Lipsen once served as advance man for President Johnson when the latter traveled to Nicaragua shortly after Sirhan Sirhan had assassinated Bobby Kennedy. Lipsen's task was to do something about the large Arab population, rumored to contain fanatics who hated Johnson. Lipsen, Bob Hardesty (a presidential aide), and Ron Pontius (a secret service agent) met with Nicaragua's military chief to discuss what to do.

> "I don't know that there is much we can do," the Nicaraguan said in accented English. "Of course," he added, "we can simply round up all the Arabs in the city and detain them until your President has departed."
>
> "I don't think we can allow that," Hardesty said. But I kicked him under the table and interjected, "That sounds fine, sir, just fine." Pontius nodded his agreement.

Later, Hardesty told me I was crazy. "We can't approve that kind of thing, Chuck," he said. "You just don't go around arresting people for no reason."

"Not in our country, you don't," I agreed. "But this isn't the United States. I sure as hell hate dictatorships, but there are times when they are damned expedient." (P. 152)

Lipsen's ability to accept dubious, even unsavory, behavior in others contrasts strikingly with the obligation participant's self-righteous stress on personal integrity. This type of participant would be shocked by Lipsen's moral relativism.

Occasionally, game participants realize that their lack of an ideological anchor may make them a party to pointless or even destructive practices. Lipsen, for example, reports having such misgivings during the Vietnam turmoil:

During 1969, I began feeling for the first time that my life was somehow out of control. Until then, I had been a political mechanic, working to add bits and pieces to the governmental engine without ever really looking to see what the whole car looked like or caring in what direction it was going to run.

Now it seemed the car was moving in an erratic circle. Not only did I feel helpless to stop it, I felt forlorn at having somehow contributed to its faulty workmanship. The system didn't seem to be working. (P. 175)

However, the game type gives but fleeting attention to the question of ultimate purposes in politics. He is too preoccupied with engaging in the daily combat. Lipsen, for example, says nothing more about the direction in which the "whole car" moves. He offers no diagnoses about the root cause of the problems; he suggests no remedies or reforms to correct the situation. He is content to continue as a "political mechanic."

Despite an apparently lax moral outlook, the game participant observes, and expects others to observe, certain basic principles of conduct. Indeed, politics would lose interest for him if these principles were broken consistently. They include (1) restraining egotism in the interest of collective purpose (being a team player); (2) not engaging in personal accusations; and (3) keeping one's word.

Like Hart, Lipsen puts special stress on this last principle. As a young man, he was instructed on this point by Sam Rayburn:

> "And," he added, sternly pointing a finger at me, "never lie. If you take a shit on the fourth floor of the Cannon Office Building, everyone will know about it on the first floor fifteen minutes later."
>
> The same, however, was true for congressmen. When they made a commitment to another member or to a lobbyist on how they would vote on a bill, they were expected to stick to it. (P. 114)

For Lipsen, lying to others becomes one of the worst faults a politician can commit. He berates Jack Kennedy because more than once "his word proved to be less than binding" (p. 130). In one incident he is outraged at Kennedy: "the bastard had given his word and he was about to break it" (p. 132). When Kennedy finally keeps his original pledge of support, Lipsen is mollified:

> It had taken some doing, but he had kept his word, even at the risk of losing support from the building trades. That's really all I ever asked from a politician. And when he came through for me, it was vitally important. (P. 133)

Keeping one's word, developing a reputation for reliability and trustworthiness: for Lipsen, as for Hart, these are vital rules that give coherence and structure to the game. To be sure, they have instrumental value. Lipsen tells us that if you were to lie to a congressman, "he would spread the word that you couldn't be trusted—and you could kiss your career good-by" (p. 114).

Nevertheless, the game participant does not keep his word simply because it is in his interest to do so. He believes deeply that this principle is correct. It is a central rule for the game of politics. Its violation destroys that game. Lipsen, for instance, tells of an occasion when he himself lied to Sam Rayburn at the Democratic Convention of 1956 and thereby achieved an enormous victory, the nomination of his candidate, Estes Kefauver, for vice president. Yet this triumph caused more personal anguish than elation:

> After the flush of victory had left me, I had misgivings. I had been a fraud. I had lied. Not to just anyone, mind you, but to the powerful and revered Speaker Sam Rayburn. It became for me a hollow victory of the spirit. (P. 87)

For the game participant, fair play is the central norm of politics. When he or others do not abide by the rules, the game no longer seems fun.

To complete our portrait of Lipsen as a game type, we note his failure to dwell upon substantive policy issues. He does, of course, write about issues. But when he does, it is only to give the reader enough background to understand the ins and outs of some involved tactical battle. Often a line or two suffices to provide the setting of the issue. Then pages may be devoted to the strategy of working for or against that issue.

In one case, for instance, Lipsen tells about the time he invented a bill of his own:

> I drew up a bill called the poison prevention packaging law which would require manufacturers of drugs and medicines to devise bottle caps with special safety features making them next to impossible for children to open. (P. 162)

He found a senator and a representative to sponsor this bill, worked to push it through both Houses of Congress, and actually saw it enacted. Exactly one short paragraph is devoted to the substance of the bill. Then follow two pages describing the clever tactics he employed to get the bill passed and the lessons he learned as a result of his action. The focus of interest is clearly on strategy, not policy.

This is not to say that game types ignore or are poorly informed on issues. Indeed, the opposite may be true. Issues are a central part of the political game. The strong competitor studies issues and develops forceful arguments to serve his side in the inevitable struggles over policy matters. But a game type like Lipsen does not participate in order to take positions on policy issues. He takes positions in order to play the game.

7 The Mission and Adulation Incentives

THE FIVE INCENTIVE TYPES examined in the preceding pages — status, program, conviviality, obligation, and game — are the only ones we have encountered in the United States. From our work in foreign settings, however, we know of two other incentives; we call them "mission" and "adulation." These types are important in some countries. We shall summarize them here to complete the picture of incentives. The reader who wishes to learn more about these incentives may consult the studies in which they are examined more fully.[1]

The *mission incentive* is the need to be committed to a transcendental cause that gives meaning and purpose to life. This drive is closely akin to a religious need; one can go far in understanding mission participants by treating them as devout adherents to a religious sect. What sets the mission type apart from the devotee of a normal religion is the nature of his belief. Normal religions are spiritual, focused on a realm distinct from the real world. The mission participant's religion is secular. The real world is the arena in which the transcendental cause is fought for and realized. The mission participant places his heaven on earth; naturally, therefore, he finds himself drawn into politics to work toward this utopia.

In an interview, what distinguishes the mission participant is the stress he places on the doctrine or ideology of his group. He refers to it repeatedly as the basis on which he interprets events, and as the basis for his own behavior.

Significantly, he may have little understanding of this doctrine. He may be unable to discuss it; he may be reluctant to analyze it. To an outsider the "doctrine" may seem banal, foolish, or vague to the point of not deserving the name of "doctrine." None of this matters to the mission participant. His need is an emotional one: to believe that there is an overall answer to his anxieties about ultimate purpose and value. He does not need to know specific details of this ideological system.

In fact, to a considerable extent, the mission type prefers to avoid delving into the doctrine to which he is committed. Such personal explorations may reveal gaps and contradictions that would sap his conviction that the doctrine accounts perfectly for everything. Consequently, mission types generally exhibit an orientation of intellectual subservience. They venerate the top leader-ideologists of their movement as great thinkers, as high priests capable of discerning the fine points of doctrine that only confuse and unsettle lesser minds. When asked to explain tactics and immediate goals, they point toward these leaders. They view themselves as humble servants of the transcendental cause. They resist thinking independently: "The party has decided" is typically given as the basis for their opinions.

Mission participants are emotionally most threatened by challenges to the transcendental character of their doctrine. They are generally distressed by any circumstance that suggests their doctrine is not the source of absolute truth. In arguments challenging their faith, for example, they are extremely dogmatic and nonempirical; they explain away contradictions with rationalizations that, to the outsider, often seem silly or incredibly twisted.

This same anxiety about preserving the transcendental status of their doctrine makes mission participants deeply distressed by the existence of a parallel group with an apparently similar doctrine. The existence of such a group suggests the doctrine is mutable and subjective, and therefore its truth is not self-evident. As a result, mission participants are intensely hostile toward groups that claim the same ideology. (They, of course, insist it is not the same but a perversion or corruption of the "true" faith.)

On the other hand, circumstances that dramatize the validity of their doctrine are exhilarating to mission types. The correctness and value of the doctrine are strengthened in times of crisis. Political and economic collapse, for example, are invigorating to (out of power) mission participants because such events "prove" the need for their doctrine. We speculate that such times of crisis probably lead to the production of mission types in a country.

In a similar fashion, repression exhilarates mission participants: as evil looms larger, the doctrine of salvation glows more brightly. We speculate that the attempted suppression of groups of mission participants will tend to increase their numbers; the "coddling" of mission types, as would typically happen in the United States, will undermine their zeal.

Mission types are often "extremists," advocating a new social order. We have found mission participants predominating in the French Communist party; it appears that Marxist movements generally attract this type.[2] But one should be careful not to make too close an equation between this incentive and a revolutionary orientation. We have found some mission types — among Gaullists in France and among Christian Socialists in the Dominican Republic — who are committed to democratic and nonviolent ideals. Furthermore, other types of participants — obligation, status, adulation — may be, or appear to be, dogmatic idealists or committed revolutionaries.

The *adulation incentive* is the need for exaggerated praise and affection. The adulation participant wants to be loved; he wants to experience the outpouring of popular gratitude. This incentive may be described as combining some features of the status incentive with some features of the conviviality incentive. Like the status type, the adulation participant is highly egocentric, forceful, and self-confident. Like the status type, he craves external evidence of his personal worth. But the type of evidence of worth he seeks is different. The adulation participant wants personal, human reinforcement. He wants people to acclaim him, praise him, thank him. Interviews with this type are laden with reports about experiences documenting personal popularity and claims of popular trust. The status type, in contrast, responds to formal, societal measures of worth: prizes, degrees, positions, mentions in newspapers and history books. The adulation type is uninterested in these formal status symbols; he wants the palpable, physical approval of live human beings.

The adulation participant also differs sharply from the status type in the perspective he has on his own career. Adulation types are uncalculating. They are strongly swayed by their immediate needs for acclaim; they do not engage in long-range planning of their careers. Because they need to believe in their own appeal, they downplay the importance of strategies and techniques of self-advancement. If they win an election, for example, they believe it is simply because they are most loved by the people. They do not want to view such contests—as status types do—as decided by strategems, hard work, propaganda techniques, and luck. Such a calculating, cynical perspective robs the victory of its adulation content.

The adulation participant resembles the conviviality type in being preoccupied with direct, personal approval. But the tone and texture of this preoccupation are quite different. The conviviality type is shy and hesitant. He seeks only to be accepted into a group, not to be the leader. The adulation participant wants to be at stage center, garnering the applause of the audience. He is forceful and strongly—even outrageously—self-confident.

The conviviality type is sensitive, alert to the feelings of others; the adulation participant is more thoroughly self-centered, unmindful of the perspectives others may have in viewing him. For example, adulation types readily brag about their virtues and popularity. Conviviality participants, sensitive that others might be "turned off," avoid direct self-praise.

Adulation participants are distinctive in being acutely preoccupied with their own self-image of integrity. In interviews they repeatedly insist that they are honest and never tell lies, as if the interviewer had challenged them on the point. This preoccupation reflects their need to hold a high self-image, to believe themselves genuinely worthy of adulation.

The adulation participant has, despite his robust exterior, an extremely thin skin. He is wounded deeply by instances of adulation denial: criticism, opposition, ostracism. Conviviality types are wounded by such disapproval, too, but being cautious and sensitive in their search for social acceptance, they generally avoid making a hostile reaction to criticism. Adulation types are not conflict avoiders. They drive forcefully and recklessly for pinnacles of acclaim, they collide with others, and, typically, they reap antagonism. As a result, politics among such participants is embittered and volatile.

In explaining the adulation incentive, we have theorized that it traces to a cultural condition we call "affection-consciousness." In the affection-conscious society, great importance attaches to garnering the warmth and praise of others. When this preoccupation with affection characterizes a society, then politicians with this orientation—adulation types—will be common.[3]

The United States lacks this social condition of affection-consciousness, and, for this reason, we believe, the adulation incentive is virtually nonexistent here. In other developed countries as well, we see little sign of adulation types. In some underdeveloped countries, on the other hand, the adulation incentive is quite common. In the Dominican Republic, where the society is markedly affection-conscious, politicians with an adulation incentive are the most common type. Brazil is another country where adulation types have been found.[4] Some clues suggest that the adulation incentive may be important in some countries of the Mideast and Africa.

8 Incentives and Political Behavior

HOW DO INCENTIVES SHAPE the behavior of politicians? Thus far in this book we have not addressed this question. Our purpose has been to describe the incentive types and their different characteristics. A proper exploration of the relationship between incentives and behavior belongs in another place. Indeed, it belongs in many other places, for, in the end, incentive analysis applies to a wide range of topics in politics.

However, we would not like to leave the subject of incentive applications entirely untouched. Incentive analysis is a significant approach to many political questions. While a comprehensive account is beyond the scope of this book, it is possible here to summarize some general observations about the use and significance of incentive analysis. Our aim in the following pages is not to emphasize particular findings, but to give a brief overview of the importance of incentives in shaping political processes and institutions.

Incentives do influence the behavior of politicians. Politicians face, day by day, minute by minute, an endless stream of choices about activities, strategies, and goals. In many of these choices, incentives will play a role. One alternative will more likely gratify a politician's incentive than another alternative. Incentives stand, then, as motivational guides: a politician will tend to behave in ways consistent with the gratification of his incentive.

It follows that we should be able to predict the behavior of a politician from a knowledge of his incentive. We know the needs, orientations, and impulses of each incentive type. From this knowledge, we can hypothesize what the tendency of each type will be in a given situation.

Of course, incentives are not the only element in the makeup of a politician. Politicians are complex human beings, each with idiosyncratic traits, attitudes, and abilities. These many other features of character and intellect also have a bearing on the choices the politician makes. Consequently, an incentive-based prediction of behavior cannot be expected to hold for each individual case. An incentive hypothesis is an "everything else being equal" statement. It identifies a general tendency that would be manifest in the average case; in any given case, this tendency might easily be overridden by other factors.

For this reason, incentive analysis is aimed at the behavior of groups of politicians, rather than the behavior of a single individual. In groups, the idiosyncratic factors governing behavior will tend to cancel out, leaving an average tendency for incentives to explain. If applied to an individual, incentive analysis would help us understand some orientations and characteristics, but used alone it would give an incomplete picture of the politician.

Incentive predictions, then, are probabilistic statements. Though they are derived with the individual in mind, they are tested at the group level. In incentive analysis, our attention is not upon what Senator Smith will do. Our interest lies in statements that predict, for example, how a group of senators with a conviviality incentive will behave. This focus on groups represents a limitation of incentive analysis, but it also reveals a strength. Political processes and institutions, we believe, are shaped by what large numbers of participants do over a period of time. The focus on group behavior, then, makes incentive analysis appropriate for the exploration of broad questions about political practices around the world.

To give the reader an idea of how incentive analysis is pursued, it might be helpful to summarize a specific case. For many years, we have been studying the incentives of members of legislative bodies. Our interest has been drawn, particularly, to legislators with a status incentive.

Consider, first, the making of general speeches in the legislature. The status type, we know, is oriented toward publicity. He enjoys being the center of attention. The idea of going down in history, enshrined in the record, would appeal to him. From this understanding of status-type characteristics, we reach the prediction that status types are more likely to engage in general floor speaking than are other types. In several instances we have tested this hypothesis, and it has been confirmed in each case.[1]

Closely related to speech making is publicity seeking. We reason that status types, given their drive for public recognition, would be energetic publicity seekers. In addition, status type are most preoccupied with career advancement. Therefore, they should be more energetic than other incentive types in seeking publicity for career-related reasons. We have made a number of separate studies of the newspaper coverage of U.S. congressmen and senators, and we find this expectation consistently supported: status types get more coverage.[2]

Status types are keenly interested in career advancement and publicity, but they are not especially interested in the substance of policy. Even when they are "ideological" position takers, they do not—as we saw in the case of William Jennings Bryan—care deeply about the substance and details of policy. From this observation, we derive the prediction that status types will be relatively inactive in the nonpublicized phases of legislative policymaking. For example, we would expect them to be poor attenders at committee hearings where much of the substance of legislative policy making is conducted. This hypothesis has been tested both for French deputies and U.S. representatives, and it has been confirmed in both cases.³ Incidentally, we would expect that for the occasional highly publicized committee hearing, the status types would be more likely to attend. Again, the data support this expectation.⁴

Status types also differ in their attitude toward legislative decorum. There are a number of reasons to suppose that, more than most other politicians, status types are inclined to be disruptive in their behavior. First, they are more anxious for the publicity that conflict-provoking activity can bring; accusations, exaggerations, and histrionics attract media coverage. Second, status types tend to be more partisan and subjective, insensitive to opposing arguments and perspectives. Therefore, they are more easily provoked to indignation. Finally, status types suffer least from disruption; a conflict-ridden environment does not much interfere with the gratification of their needs. Other incentive types have needs that are served by a stable, orderly climate. The conviviality type wants harmony and good feeling. The game type wants a "fair" game in which conflict is depersonalized. And the program type wants an orderly, rational policy making process. These participants would refrain from disorderly conduct so as not to create a situation that would interfere with their own drives and satisfactions. The needs of the status type are not contradicted by a disruptive climate; hence, these participants are less inhibited in creating such a climate.

One test of this disruptiveness hypothesis was performed on French deputies. An examination was made of the frequency with which deputies made and provoked interruptions in general floor debate. The results confirm our expectation: the status types were more disruptive.⁵

We have arrived at and, in many cases, tested, other hypotheses about the behavior of status types in legislative bodies. These hypotheses cover not only their behavior as legislators but also many aspects of their career patterns. For example, we have found that status types enter politics at an earlier age, and reach any given office at a younger age, than other types.[6] This relationship has been subjected to many validation tests, both direct and indirect, and has been supported consistently.[7] Hence, young entry age can be used as a rough method of identifying politicians with a status incentive. Other career patterns can also be used as indirect measures of the status incentive: status types are more likely than others to try for higher office; they are less likely to have local legislative experience.[8] Such indirect measures are useful when the direct measure, the personally focused interview, is beyond reach — as it would be, for example, if one wished to study past generations of politicians.

Although we have given status-type legislators the most attention, we have also studied legislators with other incentives. Again, we have found differences in behavior that are consistent with the incentives of different legislators.[9] Beyond legislative bodies, there are many other contexts in which incentive analysis can be applied. How do the different incentive types behave in political parties? In administrative positions? In judicial posts? As election campaigners? The explorations we have made in these areas indicate that the orientations and behavior of the different incentive types vary considerably.

INSTITUTIONAL CONTRASTS AND INSTITUTIONAL CHANGE

While it is interesting to hypothesize about and document relationships between incentive types and behavior, such analyses are really only a preliminary step. Lying beyond the differences in behavior of the incentive types are the differences in institutions caused by incentives. If the members of one body have different incentives from members of another body, this difference in incentives will give rise to different practices and norms. Imagine, for example, a legislature composed only of status types, and another legislature composed only of program types. The difference in incentives would give rise to different orientations, different aims, and different patterns of behavior. Over the long run, as the participants had time to adjust the institution to suit them, the difference in incentives would result in different rules, procedures, and functions.

In the institutions we find around the country and around the world, it often happens that different proportions of each incentive type are present. Why these differences occur is itself a large topic in incentive analysis. Sometimes one can point to specific features in the culture that cause one or another incentive to be prevalent.[10] Differences in the mechanisms whereby officials are recruited is another common source of variation in incentive proportions. That is, a recruitment system may screen out some incentive types and screen in others.[11] Another cause of incentive variations is the attractiveness of the institution for the different incentive types. Depending on its function and character, an institution may especially attract one incentive type and repel another.

Whatever their source, differences in incentive composition will result in differences in the processes and performance of institutions. Groups, organizations, and institutions will tend to operate in a fashion consistent with the dominant incentive of their members. To explain why an institution is the way it is — or why it differs from another body — one should look for differences in incentives. Of course, incentives will not be the complete explanation of institutional differences. Every institution operates in a restricted setting: other institutions, legal arrangements, and cultural conditions influence it. But insofar as it is free to arrange its practices, an institution will be shaped by the incentives of its members.

To illustrate how incentives may be used to explain institutional patterns, we may return to our illustration of a legislature dominated by status types. The illustration given earlier was hypothetical, but in Colombia, South America, such a legislature actually exists. In that country, the status incentive is clearly the predominant one—both for politicians in general and for deputies and senators.[12] Knowing what we know about the behavioral tendencies of status types in legislatures, we can explain the characteristics of the Colombian Congress.

First, floor debate is the central activity, consuming more time than any other legislative activity, such as committee meetings. This debate is often disruptive, characterized by acrimonious attacks, posturing, and deliberately instigated physical violence (called *zambra*). Spectators in the galleries are permitted—actually encouraged—to cheer or shout down speakers. Little attention is given to the substance of policy making. There are few committees and their meetings are poorly attended. Neither in committees nor in floor sessions is legislation examined closely; Congress generally approves only the outlines of a measure, leaving the executive branch to write the full law. As the reader can see, the nature of this institution follows from the behavioral tendencies of status-type legislators.[13]

Incentives help account for differences among institutions; they also can explain changes in one institution over time. The proportion of the different incentive types in a body often varies from one period to another. Any number of circumstances—a change in recruitment system, a generational shift, a political upheaval—may produce an alteration in the proportions of different incentive types in an institution. As a result, the institution will tend to be changed to conform to the new mix of incentives.

One such change appears to have occurred in the U.S. House of Representatives. From the mid-1950s to the present, the proportion of status types has apparently increased substantially. A change in the system of selecting congressmen seems to underlie this shift in incentives. The recruitment system for congressmen became more "democratic" during this period. Both primary and general elections opened up. Gone were the bosses and party machines that controlled nominations and elections; candidates were more often left to fend for themselves in strenuous mass popularity contests. The status type, with his greater ambition and greater publicity skills, was thus favored by the rise of such contests. An examination of indirect measures of the presence of status types supports this theory: the entry stage of congressmen dropped sharply over this period, and the proportion of House members quitting to run for higher office increased.[14]

This increase in the proportion of status types has, we believe, led to many of the recent changes in the House. For example, the publicity-seeking impulse of status types helps account for the increase in the number of floor speeches; for the growth of newsletters, TV taping facilities, and congressional PR staff; for the full admission of broadcast media into committee hearings in the late 1960s; for the virtual disappearance of closed-door hearings by the early 1970s; and for the rise in attention-getting, scandal-oriented committee hearings. The oft-noticed demise of the apprenticeship norm (freshmen congressmen should be silent and observe) is readily explained by the rise in status types: status types do not like to be silent.[15]

One might say that the U.S. House is coming to resemble the Colombian Congress—and for the same reason: status types are shaping the norms and practices of the institution. Perhaps the reader now understands the attention we have devoted to the behavior of status types. We are apprehensive about the future.

POLITICAL STABILITY

Why do some governments function smoothly and why are others in turmoil? Why does an open, democratic system sur-

Incentives and Political Behavior 177

vive in some places and collapse into dictatorship elsewhere? Incentive analysis has much to contribute in answering such fundamental questions.

Some incentives lead politicians to behave in ways conducive to political instability; other incentives do not. The stability of a system, then, will be affected by the proportions of the different incentives among its participants.

One incentive that is destabilizing, for example, is status. We may briefly review the status-type orientations that lead to instability.

1. The need for publicity causes status types to indulge in criticism, exaggeration, and scapegoating in order to attract attention to themselves. In this way, they provoke and exacerbate conflicts, setting class against class and party against party. Furthermore, this pattern of criticism and exposé fosters distrust of governmental institutions and brings governmental leaders into disrepute. Hence, overthrowing these leaders and institutions is encouraged.

2. Strong ambition for office leads status types to bend or break norms of fair play in order to achieve personal success. In office, status types are tempted to use the governmental apparatus to trammel opponents who seek to displace them. Out of power, status types encourage activity designed to embarrass and topple incumbents. They instigate street demonstrations aimed at violence; they encourage strikes that cause disruption in daily life; they may even abet arsonists, thieves, and kidnappers. Even petty forms of rule-breaking — heckling speakers, irregularities in voter registration — are pernicious. When widely practiced, these disruptions produce a vicious circle of recrimination and retaliation that sets the stage for violence and major disruption of the constitutional system.

3. Not being deep or careful thinkers on policy matters, status types are likely to enact measures that are popularly appealing but counterproductive in the long run. Naturally, the

deleterious effects of these policies will lead the public to conclude that the government is incompetent and deserves to be displaced.

Perhaps the most common theme of governmental mismanagement around the world lies in the fiscal and monetary realm. It is superficially appealing to issue governmental benefits to the populace and superficially appealing not to raise taxes to pay for such benefits. The shortsighted handling of fiscal affairs leads, then, to bankruptcy or monetary debasement and inflation. These economic difficulties cause, in turn, social conflict and hostility directed at the government.

Political instability, then is brought about by a combination of three elements: (1) widespread criticism and scapegoating; (2) infringements of norms of fair play; (3) the adoption of policies appealing in the short run but injurious in the long run. Status-type politicians tend to behave in a way that will give rise to all three conditions. Also, for reasons we shall not explain here, adulation and mission types tend to produce the same three conditions. Hence, we would expect that where any of these three incentives are predominant, a tendency toward instability will result. Exactly what form that instability might take could vary, depending on local circumstances. It might be terrorism, military coups, or the forced resignation of a president. But some form of turmoil or constitutional irregularity is to be expected.

On the other hand, the orientations of program, game, and conviviality participants lead away from the conditions fostering instability. These three types are not personally anxious to attract publicity; therefore, they are less likely to engage in extensive criticism and scandal mongering. All three types have an incentive-based interest in seeing that rules are not bent or broken. The program type wants an orderly, rational policy making system to work within; the game type wants a structured, predictable setting for the game he enjoys; the conviviality type wants the limitation of personal friction ensured by adherence to rules.

Game and, especially, program types take a deeper, more responsible view of policy making than do other politicians. Hence, they are less likely to enact shortsighted and destructive measures. Conviviality types are not oriented this way; they are as disposed to favor superficially appealing measures as are status types. But a system in which conviviality types predominated would probably not be unstable. While they might adopt policies injurious to their countries, conviviality types would not engage in vigorous criticism or in rule breaking. Hence, these two ingredients causing instability would be absent.

It will take many years to explore and test this broad theory of political instability. We offer it here not as a finished conclusion, but as an illustration of a new avenue of inquiry opened up by incentive analysis. We do not suppose that a complete theory of political instability can rest on incentives alone. There are a number of institutional and circumstantial conditions that would have to be included in a complete analysis. But it does seem that an effort to account for political instability will be inadequate if it ignores the character of the politicians themselves.

Concluding Observations

Theories about the behavior of politicians rest upon assumptions about the motivations of these politicians. Whenever one reasons that politicians will do this or that in a given situation, one works from assumptions about their goals and orientations. Why not, we argue, make these assumptions explicit? Why not learn what motivations actually exist and then do our reasoning in terms of these empirical findings? This is the case for incentive analysis.

In the past, political analyses have typically handled the motivational issue after the fashion of economics, by the introduction of assumptions about formal goals. Politicians are assumed to be maximizing a specific objective, or possibly a combination of objectives. While this "formal goal" approach has utility for handling certain problems, it is, we believe, an inadequate approach to most topics in political analysis. Our criticism of formal goal assumptions is not, primarily, that such assumptions are often inaccurate. Our objection runs deeper: formal goals, even if correctly identified, are too superficial to explain most significant political behavior.

In pursuing any goal, or combination of goals, the politician is faced with thousands of day-to-day choices, choices about what tactics and strategy he should follow, what role he should play, what style and tone he should adopt. In making these choices, formal goals give little guidance. Except in rare cases, the politician cannot know—nor can we—which choice will fulfill these goals. Any goal may be pursued in a number of different ways.

Consider, for example, the commonly used assumption that politicians seek to hold office or seek to win reelection. What will this assumption explain about the behavior of, say, legislators? There being no certain way to succeed and no certain way to fail, everyone is free to adopt his own theories. Will making speeches in the legislative chamber pay off electorally? Will socializing personally with constituents? Will hard work in committees? Does mudslinging in campaigns help or hurt? Will acting as a spokesman for special interest groups aid one's chances of reelection? Is accepting a bribe worth the risk? Should the candidate project an image of being outraged at injustice or of being aloof from battle, or of being kind to children? Perhaps berating constituents aids reelection; even this approach has been tried successfully on occasion. In short, a wide range of strategies, tactics, roles, and styles are arguably consistent with the goal of reelection. What, then, do we explain by imputing this goal to politicians? The shallowness of formal goal explanations is often overlooked because analysts generally use these explanations post hoc. They observe what happens and then, afterwards, argue that this behavior is consistent with the assumption that participants seek to maximize votes or their tenure in office. What these observers fail to realize is that the same assumption can be appealed to in order to explain many different patterns of behavior. Formal goals can be pursued through an almost infinite variety of behaviors: knowing the goal will not enable us to predict the behavior.

To take another illustration of this point, consider policy goals. Even if we assume that policy aims are primary motives, what will knowing a policy goal tell us about the behavior of participants who have it? Will they work quietly through the legislature, the administration, or the courts? Will they stress mass publicity? Will they employ street demonstrations? Will they resort to terrorism and assassinations? Will they form a political party, or any type of organization? Will such organizations be cohesive and hierarchical? Will these participants work closely with other groups with similar aims? Will they maintain a working relationship with their opponents?

Perhaps most important is the character of their policy goals. Will these participants want symbolic benefits or concrete changes? Will they want public credit, or will they be content to allow others to appear to put their policies into effect? Will they view their policy aims in a short-run, superficial perspective, or will they adopt a comprehensive approach? And how will they evaluate the success of their efforts: Will they be subjective, always assuming the problem persists no matter what is done, or will they rely on objective data about the problem they seek to solve?

The answers to such questions do not follow from assuming or knowing that participants have a particular policy goal.

Given the same policy objective, participants can adopt a wide variety of tactics, styles, and organizational arrangements. And the users of each tactic will defend it as the best method to implement the goal. Imagine, for example, that Benjamin Franklin and William Jennings Bryan were placed in the same setting and given the same policy goal. Would assuming that they both sought, let us say, to found a local hospital tell us much about their behavior? Could we conclude that they would employ the same tactics and adopt the same style?

At best, goal assumptions tell us where politicians are heading; they will not account for the route they choose, or for what they do along the way. Explaining politics in terms of formal goals is like accounting for the work of Michelangelo by saying his goal was "to make pictures and statues." Such a statement is true as far as it goes, but it says nothing important. Strategies, tactics, roles, and styles are politics. It is what we see in legislative chambers, in administrative offices, and in the streets.

The politician is not locked into a pattern of behavior by any particular goal. He is relatively free to choose his own approach, his own style, and his own mix of tactics. His choices will be governed by his needs and orientations. To some extent, these needs and orientations will be the outgrowth of unique features of his personality; but, to a degree, they will also reflect his incentive. The incentive approach, then, affords a different, and we think more realistic, starting point for theorizing about political behavior. It focuses upon the impulses that lead politicians to choose different styles and strategies.

There are no fixed relationships between means and ends in politics. There are too many imponderables—too much complexity, too many unknowns, too many accidental factors—to permit anyone to deduce logically the optimal path to a given end. Everyone sees through a glass darkly. Participants themselves are notoriously subjective in groping about for instrumentalities. Politicians professing common goals repeatedly dispute with each other about approaches, about strategy, and about intermediate goals — and typically end up going their separate ways. Politics is not an exact pursuit in which tactics can be logically derived from goals, and goals can be logically derived from the objective context.

Politics is a gong show. The stage is open to any member of the audience to come up and do his thing. It is personality that governs why some people seek to be on the stage, and it is personality that shapes the kind of act they put on. If we seek to understand this spectacle, we must explore the personalities of the participants.

Appendix I

Outline of Incentive Characteristics as Seen in Interviews

STATUS TYPE

a. He stresses the following themes: personal career; experiences involving personal advancement (such as past campaigns); tactics and techniques of advancement (such as generating publicity, projecting an image, and campaigning).

b. He makes more than normal mention of offices held, career dates, awards, and other status symbols, and he frequently refers to others in status terms ("higher or lower," "distinguished," "prestigious," etc.).

c. He frequently refers to status values: fame, honor, awards, success, importance, etc.

d. He tends to be cynical in his attitude toward other politicians, seeing them as calculating and opportunistic; he may be quite bitter and hostile toward others.

e. He is defensive about criticism and antagonistic toward critics.

f. He values personal loyalty and laments being "betrayed" by others.

g. He values his own independence, that is, not being "beholden" to other persons or forces.

h. He tends to place himself above others, as one who is looked up to for leadership.

i. In policy discussions, he tends to use popular clichés and abstract generalities, that give the appearance of sophistication; he avoids concrete aspects and details of policy questions.

j. He tends to be subjective and partisan in evaluating opponents and opposing arguments.

k. Insofar as policy matters are mentioned, he stresses his own involvement, neglecting the objective analysis of the policy problem itself.

l. In the interview situation, he tends to lack candor. He evades probing questions and attempts to create an "impression." A tension with interviewer often develops as the subject resists the dependent role of interviewee. Interview tends to be shorter than normal, often terminated by the subject.

PROGRAM TYPE

a. He stresses the following themes: the substance of policy issues; the rationality and efficiency of policy making procedures; "small" policy questions, concrete details, specific illustrations.

b. He is preoccupied with the cause-and-effect, factual analysis of policy problems.

c. He avoids symbolic position taking; he avoids general-level policy discussions; he avoids clichés.

d. He is objective, recognizing opposing arguments.

e. He is open-minded, not absolutist or dogmatic about his views.

f. He displays a concern for the accuracy and meaningfulness of the facts and figures he cites; he avoids exaggeration; he stresses the importance of information.

g. He exhibits a positive, approving attitude toward other politicians; his disagreements with others are expressed matter of factly; he exhibits little personal irritation or hostility.

h. He values maintaining harmonious "working" relationships with others, including opponents.

i. He tends to view politics as a hobby, not as a career or a crusade; he sees other, nonpolitical, enterprises as providing equivalent challenges for him.

j. He is uninterested in the mechanics of position getting (campaigning, publicity tactics, etc.).

k. He is often iconoclastic in contradicting popular beliefs by pointing out little-recognized facts and arguments.

l. In the interview situation, he is candid and frank, and very talkative about policy issues.

CONVIVIALITY TYPE

a. He stresses the following themes: participating in convivial interactions; liking people; being liked by people; being helpful to others; being sensitive to the feelings of others.

b. He talks much about other people and their activities; he tends to treat himself as a spectator.

c. He views his social environment as harmonious and friendly.

d. He tends to avoid reporting conflictive situations involving himself; when he does mention such conflicts, he views them as disturbing and uncomfortable.

e. He may report having stood up against others on occasion, but such minor claims contradict the larger picture of him as one who goes along, as a conflict avoider.

f. He tends to avoid specific criticism of others and is restrained and oblique in referring to his dislikes.

g. He readily and warmly praises political colleagues and superiors.

h. He expresses little in the way of policy views; the policy discussion he does offer is characterized by little depth.

i. He expresses doubts about his own abilities and appears to lack self-confidence. He tends to be hesitant and to understate (using the modifier "little," for example). He engages in self-deprecation.

j. His conversation tends to be rambling and digressive, as if he has no clear point to pursue but is just making conversation.

k. In the interview situation, he is polite, responsive to the interviewer, not forceful. He may be either jovial and relaxed, or rather shy and ill at ease.

OBLIGATION TYPE

a. He stresses the following themes: doing the right thing; following one's conscience; doing one's duty; following moral and ethical principles; being fair, consistent, and conscientious.

b. He persistently adopts a normative, "should-ought" perspective on almost all topics.

c. He values honesty and integrity; he disapproves of self-seeking, of compromising one's principles, and of seeking to be popular instead of doing the right thing.

d. He reports his entry into politics in obligation terms, as arising out of a sense of duty.

e. He readily and sharply criticizes others, especially for unprincipled behavior. He readily reports instances of conflict with others, especially conflicts involving his standing up for a principle.

f. He expresses hostility toward politics and politicians in general as unprincipled; he does not consider himself a "politician."

g. He expresses approval of political figures he perceives as being principled, frank, or uncompromisingly idealistic.

h. He expresses firm policy views, but his positions are one-sided, not comprehensive. He often skips rapidly from issue to issue.

i. He is often more concerned with style (proper appearance or following correct procedure) than with substantive policy outcomes.

j. He often views himself as alone, battling against the tide in the name of principle.

k. In the interview situation, he is frank, forceful, unconcerned with giving offense, and rigid and dogmatic in his style of thought and expression. He is usually highly talkative.

GAME TYPE

a. He stresses the following themes: strategy and tactics; interrelationships among political actors; competition with others; real (as opposed to formal) political structures; roles of different actors and the different perspectives they create; personalities, objectively analyzed.

b. He readily generalizes about relationships and rules of successful interaction; these generalizations are nondogmatic and empirical, often prefaced by "it depends..." (on the personality, role, situation, etc.).

c. He is keenly aware of power, defined not as prestige but as the ability to influence others.

d. He stresses, even exaggerates, the raw, Machiavellian "reality" of politics and downplays idealism, ideology, and moralism; he resists covering over this reality with euphemisms.

e. He is objective in his political analyses, rising above personal and partisan perspectives in his view of the political world.

f. He is pragmatic, accepting people and their goals as he finds them.

g. He deems important some basic principles of personal conduct: (1) keeping one's word; (2) restraining egotism in the interest of collective purposes (being a team player); and (3) not engaging in personal accusations (not playing "dirty").

h. He views politics positively; he is not cynical.

i. He readily characterizes himself as a "politician."

j. He is zestful about his activities and strongly enjoys politics; he views himself as an actor, not a spectator.

k. He respects opponents as role players entitled to attempt to defeat him (within the bounds of fair conduct).

l. He frequently employs sports terms and analogies.

m. He typically fails to dwell upon substantive policy issues in the interview.

n. In the interview situation, he is robust and self-confident, frank, open to self-analysis, and businesslike.

Appendix II

CONDUCTING AND INTERPRETING INCENTIVE INTERVIEWS

CONDUCTING THE INTERVIEW

To be useful for incentive analysis, an interview should reveal the respondent's personal feelings about politics. It should get at what he likes and dislikes about politics, at how he enjoys spending his time, at his personal hopes and apprehensions, and at his reaction to others involved in politics. In order to encourage the respondent to talk freely about these personal topics, the interviewer should strive to create a relaxed, nonthreatening atmosphere. The interviewer should not read his questions (they should be memorized); nor should he take notes during the interview. The respondent should be told that all names and identifying characteristics of individuals will be disguised if the interview is later quoted publicly. The interview should be tape-recorded, but if necessary it can be written up from memory immediately after the conclusion of the interview.

The interview should be loosely structured, so that the respondent can pursue lines of conversation that he chooses to follow. The interviewer should maintain his interest in what the respondent is saying and should probe statements with follow-up questions. It is important for the interviewer to avoid cutting off the respondent prematurely, before he has had a chance to express himself fully on a topic.

The interviewer should be genuinely interested in the respondent and in what he has to say. He should not present questions mechanically but supply appropriate introductions and transitions. The interviewer should express curiosity, surprise, or doubt just as in an ordinary conversation. Of course, the interviewer must maintain a basically neutral posture. The interviewer wants to learn what the respondent thinks; he does not want to lead the respondent, or praise him, or criticize him. He should never argue with the respondent directly; he may explore the respondent's reaction to contradiction by putting the point in the third person (e.g., "How would you respond to people who say...?").

INTERPRETING THE INTERVIEW

The recorded interview should be transcribed precisely, if possible by the person who conducted the interview. This is a tedious process, but it is vital to have an accurate transcript for subsequent analysis. Pauses and conversational filler words ("Well, I think, that is..." should be included in the transcript; "uh" and "er," etc., need not be typed.

In interpreting a transcript of an incentive interview, the analyst should first read the entire transcript in order to gain a feel for the respondent and the texture of the interview. It is important to avoid, as much as possible, forming an impression of the respondent's incentive on the basis of this initial reading; perhaps the most common pitfall in analyzing interviews is to allow a first impression to shape subsequent interpretation in such a way as to blind the analyst to material that might suggest incentives other than the preconceived one.

After the initial perusal of the transcript, the analyst should read through the interview carefully. Making use of the list of incentive characteristics given in Appendix I, he should make note of statements by the respondent that suggest one incentive or another. The analyst should reflect on the meaning of each statement or passage and should not necessarily accept everything the respondent says at face value. What is the significance of this statement? Why did he make it? What orientation does it reveal? These are the kinds of questions the analyst should ask himself.

Although considerable interpretation is necessary in analyzing an incentive interview, the procedure should be conducted as systematically as possible. We have found the following system of coding interviews to be helpful. We assign a value of one point to each statement that suggests an incentive, though not strongly; four points to statements whose substance and length point more clearly to a given incentive; and seven points to the rare statements that so strongly indicate an incentive that it would be hard to conceive of someone with another incentive giving that same response. In addition, statements that negate or argue against an incentive are given a value of minus one for the incentive negated.

The next step in this procedure is to add up all the points for and against each incentive. Most interviews will contain a smattering of material that, in a rather incidental matter, indicates a number of incentives. However, it is likely that one incentive will receive a much higher total score than any other incentive.

One method we have employed to classify interviews is "team coding." Instead of having one individual work on the interview by himself, two researchers simultaneously read, discuss, and interpret the interview transcript. The team then makes a single classification—which, for purposes of reliability, may be compared with the classifications of the same interview by teams that have worked independently.

The chief advantage of team coding is that it makes it easier to be open-minded in the interpretation process. The members of the team naturally take up pro and con positions on the evaluation of each comment. They also are in a position to share insights with each other. Moreover, the process of team coding turns out to be faster than coding by individuals. A single person needs considerable time, perhaps weeks, to struggle on his own to adopt different perspectives, develop insights, and maintain objectivity. In team coding, we find that we need only about two, two-hour sessions to arrive at a judgment: one session for a preliminary reading and a second, a few days later, for final coding.

Even when the team coding method is used, the danger still exists of falling victim to preconceptions or to a common mind set. To avoid this danger, team members must strive to play devil's advocate, proposing interpretations of comments at variance with the team's favored classification.

INTERVIEW QUESTIONS

In a typical interview (which would last about one hour) not all of the following questions need be asked. Many of them will be answered by the respondent in the course of replying to other questions. The interviewer should always probe with further questions when the respondent appears disposed to continue on a theme. The order of the questions is not important, though the interviewer should begin with nonpersonal questions such as question 1.

In the following list, we have put parentheses around role-dependent terms, which are written as if one were interviewing a city councilman. For other roles—legislator, senator, mayor—these terms would change accordingly.

1. What are the most important problems (the city council) must deal with here? What have you been doing on these issues?
2. Are you personally working on any specific issue right now? Do you have a special interest in a particular policy?
3. If a (councilman) is interested in a particular measure, how does he go about getting it accepted by (the council)? What strategy or tactics should he use?

Appendix II 195

4. What qualities does it take to be a good (councilman)? Is the general quality of (city councilmen) high?
5. How do (city council members) get along with each other? Are personal relations on (the council) harmonious? What about your relations with members of the opposition party?
6. Is there an operating code among (council members), a set of do's and don't's that people are supposed to follow? If so, what are these informal rules?
7. Have you enjoyed your work on (the council)? What aspects of it have interested you most?
8. How did you first get involved in politics? (Probe for his age when first politically active, whether his family was involved, exactly how he became active, etc.) What was your first political position? How did you like this post?
9. What would you miss most if you had to leave politics altogether?
10. In general, do you enjoy political campaigns? What aspects? Do you enjoy public speaking?
11. How do you react to people today who say that politicians are not responding to the needs of the people?
12. Would you say that you have made many friends in politics? Many enemies?
13. Do you find that you get a lot of criticism? Does it bother you?
14. Would you agree with the statement that in politics everybody is pretty much out for himself?
15. In your opinion, is it better to be right than to win in politics?
16. Many people believe that in the long run, the pragmatist will be more effective than the idealist. Would you agree?
17. Would you agree with the statement that unless you learn how to compromise, you cannot achieve anything in politics?

18. Would you agree with the statement that a politician who spends a lot of time on the details of an issue is likely to lose sight of the larger picture?
19. Overall, would you say that you have enjoyed politics? What is the most enjoyable experience you have had in politics? The least enjoyable?

END OF INTERVIEW

Always close by saying something like, "That's all the questions I have to ask. Is there anything I've left out that can help me understand (city) government? Is there any important aspect of your job that I haven't touched on?"

Notes

1. Introduction

1. Aaron Wildavsky, "The Goldwater Phenomenon: Purists, Politicians, and the Two-Party System," *The Review of Politics* 27 (Jul. 1965): 386–413.
2. James David Barber, *The Lawmakers* (New Haven: Yale Univ. Press, 1965).
3. We do not believe that the use of the simple variables (expectation of returning and activity) will produce a sharp division of incentive types. We greatly doubt that the application of these measures actually produced a clear division in Barber's sample. Our experience reveals many cases of program types (lawmakers) who do not expect to continue in politics, status types (advertisers) who do, and so on. The category most likely to produce a mixture of types is the group low on activity and low on expectation of returning. Falling into this group will be some conviviality types, some obligation types, accidental entrants with no incentives, and simply the ill or the infirm. It is not surprising to us that this category (reluctant) corresponds to no incentive type we have observed.

    In the other three categories, the separation of the incentive types by means of the measures would have been only approximate. Given this confusion, Barber was indeed perceptive in extracting these three types, the interview accounts of which conform closely to our experience with these same types.
4. Michael Maccoby, *The Gamesman* (New York: Simon and Schuster, 1977).

2. The Status Incentive

1. William Jennings Bryan and Mary Baird Bryan, *The Memoirs of William Jennings Bryan* (Chicago: John L. Winston Co., 1925). This work is actually two separate volumes: Bryan's autobiography and a biography by his wife. It is only the autobiography that we examine here. All further references to this work appear in the text.

198 NOTES

2. Louis W. Koenig, *Bryan: A Political Biography of William Jennings Bryan* (New York: G. P. Putnam's Sons, 1971), p. 12.
3. This point is made in a recent article by Tom Bethell, "Washington's World of Style," *Harper's* Jan. 1978, pp. 66-75. Bethell says that politicians who want to climb the ladder of prestige in Washington must appear to be issue oriented: "Washington insiders and such types don't wear Savile Row suits, *they wear the Issues*" (p. 69, emphasis his).
4. Richard F. Fenno, Jr. makes the same observation in "U.S. House Members in their Constituencies: An Exploration," *American Political Science Review* 71 (Sept. 1977): 883-917. After following congressmen closely during their visits to their constituencies, Fenno came to the conclusion that congressmen believe what they say: "In view of the commonly held notion that elective politicians 'talk out of both sides of their mouths'...I had expected to find members of Congress explaining their activity somewhat differently to their various constituencies... But I have found little trace of such explanatory chameleons in my travels. The House members I observed give the same explanations for their Washington activity before people who disagree with them as before people who agree with them—before nonsupporters as well as supporters, from one end to the other in the most segmented of districts" (p. 913).

3. THE PROGRAM INCENTIVE

1. In quoting the autobiography, we have relied upon the version edited by Carl Van Doren, *Benjamin Franklin's Autobiographical Writings* (New York: Viking Press, 1945). We feel this edition best combines authenticity with modern spelling and punctuation. The four segments of the autobiography may be described thus:
    I. (52 pages) covering Franklin's early life and establishment as a printer in Philadelphia (pp. 216-67 in the Van Doren volume).
    II. (18 pages) mainly covering Franklin's "project of arriving at moral perfection" (pp. 616-33).
    III. (60 pages) covering Franklin's activities, public and scientific, until the age of fifty-one (pp. 701-60).
    IV. (4 pages) a fragment Franklin was working on just before he died (pp. 779-83).

4. THE CONVIVIALITY INCENTIVE

1. Brooks Hays, *A Hotbed of Tranquility: My Life in Five Worlds* (New York: Macmillan, 1968).

2. A good example is "Casualty," *Newsweek*, Nov. 17, 1958, 30–31.
3. In another work, *A Southern Moderate Speaks* (Chapel Hill: Univ. of North Carolina Press, 1959), Hays examines the history of the civil rights issue in the 1945–1958 period. Being a historical account specifically focused on the race issue, the book is not particularly useful for incentive analysis. Nevertheless, in it one notices the predominance of conviviality themes. Hays refrains from speaking critically of anyone; he is effusive in his praise of many participants; he stresses his role as a peacemaker anxious to avoid conflict.

 His middle position on the civil rights issue was apparently influenced by his desire to avoid giving offense to either side. He felt the unkindness of Jim Crow practices and therefore favored ending discrimination. But he was reluctant to turn against his fellow white southerners. Hays made it a point to be the enemy of none and work toward good will and understanding. As a result, he had many personal friends in both camps.

 Recently, Hays has written a formal autobiography: *Politics is my Parish* (Baton Rouge: Louisiana State Univ. Press, 1981). This volume lacks the spontaneity and enthusiasm of *Hotbed of Tranquility*; it is, instead, a rather mechanical historical account in strict, chronological format. It is, therefore, not particularly useful for incentive analysis.

5. THE OBLIGATION INCENTIVE

1. Frederick L. Hackenburg, *A Solitary Parade* (New York: Thistle Press, 1929).

6. THE GAME INCENTIVE

1. Charles B. Lipsen with Stephen Lesher, *Vested Interest* (Garden City, N.Y.: Doubleday, 1977). It is perhaps significant that the assistance of a professional writer, Lesher, was instrumental in producing this book. Autobiographies by game types are exceedingly rare because, we speculate, the game type's orientation toward activity and interaction makes writing a disagreeable chore. Game types enjoy talking to others, but it appears that they dislike the solitary, sedentary discipline of writing down what they know.

7. THE MISSION AND ADULATION INCENTIVES

1. James L. Payne, *Incentive Theory and Political Process* (Lexington, Mass.: D. C. Heath, 1972); Oliver H. Woshinsky, *The French Deputy* (Lexington, Mass.: D. C. Heath, 1973).

2. Two excellent examples of autobiographies by mission participants attracted to the Communist movement are Arthur Koestler, *Arrow in the Blue* (New York: Macmillan, 1952), and Whittaker Chambers, *Witness* (New York: Random House, 1952).
3. Payne, *Incentive Theory*, chap. 5.
4. Michael P. McCullough, "The Brazilian Congress," Senior thesis, Wesleyan University, 1969.

8. INCENTIVES AND POLITICAL BEHAVIOR

1. Oliver H. Woshinsky, *The French Deputy* (Lexington, Mass., D. C. Heath, 1973), pp. 129–30; James L. Payne, "The Changing Character of American Congressmen: Some Implications for Reform," paper presented at the 1977 meeting of the Midwest Political Science Association, Chicago, pp. 16–17.
2. Payne, "Changing Character of American Congressmen," pp. 16–17; Payne, "Show Horses and Work Horses in the United States House of Representatives," *Polity* 12 (Spring 1980): 428–56; Eric P. Veblen, "National Newspaper Coverage of Members of Congress: The House of Representatives, 1973–74," paper presented at the 1978 meeting of the Southwestern Social Science Association, Houston, Tex.; Veblen, "Personal Incentives and National Newspaper Coverage of U.S. Senators and Representatives," paper presented at the 1979 meeting of the Southwestern Social Science Association, Fort Worth, Tex.
3. Woshinsky, *French Deputy*, pp. 134–36; Payne, "Show Horses and Work Horses," pp. 434–42.
4. Payne, "Show Horses and Work Horses," pp. 443–44.
5. Woshinsky, *French Deputy*, pp. 137–40. To simplify this discussion we have ignored the mission type. Our understanding of this incentive would predict, and the Woshinsky data confirm, that mission types are also unusually disruptive.
6. The "other types" referred to here are the ones commonly encountered in American politics: program, game, conviviality, and obligation. Mission participants and, to a lesser degree, adulation types also enter politics at a relatively early age.
7. James L. Payne, *Patterns of Conflict in Colombia* (New Haven, Conn.: Yale Univ. Press, 1968), pp. 103–7; James L. Payne, *Incentive Theory and Political Process: Motivation and Leadership in the Dominican Republic* (Lexington, Mass., D. C. Heath, 1972), pp. 129–35; Woshinsky, *French Deputy*, pp. 143–45; Payne, "Changing Character of American Congressmen," pp. 13–18; James L. Payne, "The Personal Electoral Advantage of House Incumbents 1936–1976," *American*

Politics Quarterly 8 (Oct. 1980): 472–74; Veblen, "National Newspaper Coverage," pp. 14–21; Veblen, "Personal Incentives," pp. 11–19. Other researchers, while not specifically employing the incentive variable, have also noted the tendency for the ambitious, publicity-seeking participants to be younger. See Leo M. Snowiss, "Congressional Recruitment and Representation," *American Political Science Review* 60 (Sept. 1966): 633–36; Donald R. Matthews, *U.S. Senators and Their World* (Chapel Hill: Univ. of North Carolina Press, 1960), p. 64; James David Barber, *The Lawmakers* (New Haven, Conn.: Yale Univ. Press, 1965), p. 72.
8. Payne, "Show Horses and Work Horses," pp. 455–56; Payne, "Personal Electoral Advantage," pp. 9–25; Veblen, "National Newspaper Coverage," pp. 14–21; Veblen, "Personal Incentives," pp. 11–19.
9. Woshinsky, *French Deputy*, chaps. 7 and 8.
10. Analyses of this type are found in Payne, *Patterns of Conflict in Colombia*, chap. 2; Payne, *Incentive Theory*, chap. 5
11. An analysis of this type is found in Payne, "Changing Character of American Congressmen," and Payne, "Personal Electoral Advantage."
12. Payne, *Patterns of Conflict in Colombia*, chap. 2.
13. Ibid., chap. 11.
14. Payne, "Changing Character of American Congressmen'" pp. 11–15;Payne, "Personal Electoral Advantage," pp. 478–80; Payne, "The Rise of Lone Wolf Questioning in House Committee Hearings," *Polity* 14 (Summer 1982): 626–40.
15. A number of recent studies stress the orientation of the modern Congress toward publicity seeking. See David R. Mayhew, *Congress: The Electoral Connection* (New Haven, Conn.: Yale Univ. Press, 1974); Albert D. Cover, "The Advantage of Incumbency in Congressional Elections," Ph.D. dissertation, Yale Univ., 1976; Morris P. Fiorina, *Congress: Keystone of the Washington Establishment* (New Haven, Conn.: Yale Univ. Press, 1977); Herbert B. Asher, "The Changing Status of the Freshman Representative," in Norman J. Ornstein, ed., *Congress in Change* (New York: Praeger, 1975), pp. 216–39.

Bibliography

Incentive Research

Caldeira, Greg A. "Of Judicial Roles, State and Federal: Some Thoughts on How to Study Trial Judges." Paper delivered at the 1975 Law and Society Research Colloq., Buffalo, N.Y.

———. "Psychological Explanation of Decision-Making in Urban Trial Courts." Paper delivered at the 1975 meeting of the Southern Political Science Ass., Nashville, Tenn.

Coogan, William H., and Oliver H. Woshinsky. *The Science of Politics: An Introduction to Hypothesis Formation and Testing.* Appendix 3: "Incentives and Behavior Among American Congressmen." Washington, D.C.: University Press of America, 1982.

Payne, James L. "Career Intentions and Electoral Performance of Members of the U.S. House." *Legislative Studies Quarterly* 7 (Feb. 1982): 93-99.

———. "The Changing Nature of American Congressmen: Some Implications for Reform." Paper delivered at the 1977 meeting of the Midwestern Political Science Ass., Chicago, Ill.

———. *Incentive Theory and Political Process: Motivation and Leadership in the Dominican Republic.* Lexington, Mass.: D.C. Heath, 1972.

———. *Patterns of Conflict in Colombia.* New Haven, Conn.: Yale Univ. Press, 1968.

———. "The Personal Electoral Advantage of House Incumbents, 1936-1976." *American Politics Quarterly*, 8 (Oct. 1980): 465-82.

———. "The Rise of Lone Wolf Questioning in House Committee Hearings." *Polity* 14 (Summer 1982): 626-40.

———. "Show Horses and Work Horses in the United States House of Representatives." *Polity* 12 (Spring 1980): 428-56.

Payne, James L., and Oliver H. Woshinsky, "Incentives for Political Participation." *World Politics* 24 (July 1972): 518-46.

Sarat, Austin. "Judging in Trial Courts: An Exploratory Study." *Journal of Politics* 39. (May 1977): 368-98.

Veblen, Eric P. "Liberalism and National Newspaper Coverage of Members of Congress." *Polity* 14 (Fall 1981): 153-59.

———. "National Newspaper Coverage of Members of Congress: The House of Representatives, 1973-74." Paper delivered at the 1978 meeting of the Southwestern Social Science Ass., Houston, Tex.

———. "Personal Incentives and National Newspaper Coverage of U.S. Senators and Representatives." Paper delivered at the 1979 meeting of the Southwestern Social Science Ass., Fort Worth, Tex.

Woshinsky, Oliver H. "Donald Riegle and the Changing American Congress." Paper delivered at the 1980 meeting of the Northeastern Political Science Ass., New Haven, Conn.

———. *The French Deputy: Incentives and Behavior in the National Assembly.* Lexington, Mass.: D. C. Heath, 1973.

———. "How Incentives Shape Political Behavior: "The Case of French Deputies." Paper delivered at the 1973 meeting of the American Political Science Ass., New Orleans, La.

GENERAL WORKS

Almond, Gabriel A. *The Appeals of Communism.* Princeton, N.J.: Princeton Univ. Press, 1965.

Barber, James David. *The Lawmakers: Recruitment and Adaptation to Legislative Life.* New Haven, Conn.: Yale Univ. Press, 1965.

———. *The Presidential Character: Predicting Performance in the White House.* 2d ed. Englewood Cliffs, N.J.: Prentice-Hall, 1977.

Berrington, Hugh. "Review Article: The Fiery Chariot: British Prime Ministers and the Search for Love." *British Journal of Political Science* 4 (July 1974): 345-69.

Bowman, Lewis, Dennis Ippolito, and William Donaldson. "Incentives for the Maintenance of Grassroots Political Activism." *Midwest Journal of Political Science* 13 (Feb. 1969): 126-39.

Browning, Rufus P. "Businessmen in Politics: Motivation and Circumstances in the Rise to Power." Ph.D. dissertation, Yale Univ., 1960.

———. "The Interaction of Personality and Political System in Decisions to Run for Office: Some Data and a Simulation Technique." *Journal of Social Issues* 24 (July 1968): 93-110.

Browning, Rufus P., and Herbert Jacob. "Power Motivation and the Political Personality." *Public Opinion Quarterly* 28 (Spring 1964): 75-90.

Christie, Richard, and Florence L. Geis, eds. *Studies in Machiavellianism.* New York: Academic Press, 1970.

Clapp, Charles L. *The Congressman: His Work as He Sees It.* Washington, D.C.: The Brookings Institution, 1963.

Clark, Peter B., and James Q. Wilson. "Incentive Systems: A Theory of Organizations." *Administrative Science Quarterly* 6 (Sept. 1961): 129-66.

Conway, M. Margaret, and Frank B. Feigert. "Motivation, Incentive Systems, and the Political Party Organization." *American Political Science Review* 62 (Dec. 1968): 1159-73.

Davidson, Roger H. *The Role of the Congressman.* New York: Pegasus, 1969.

Dexter, Lewis Anthony. "The Representative and His District." In *New Perspectives on the House of Representatives,* edited by R. L. Peabody and N. W. Polsby. Chicago: Rand McNally, 1963.

Diamond, Irene. *Sex Roles in the State House.* New Haven, Conn.: Yale Univ. Press, 1977.

DiRenzo, Gordon J. *Personality, Power, and Politics: A Social Psychological Analysis of the Italian Deputy and His Parliamentary System.* Notre Dame, Ind.: Univ. of Notre Dame Press, 1967.

———, ed. *Personality and Politics.* Garden City, N.Y.: Doubleday, 1974.

Dodd, Lawrence C., and Bruce I. Oppenheimer, eds. *Congress Reconsidered.* New York: Praeger, 1977.

Elms, Alan C. *Personality in Politics.* New York: Harcourt, Brace, Jovanovich, 1976.

Fenno, Richard F., Jr. *Congressmen in Committees.* Boston: Little, Brown, 1973.

———. "The House Appropriations Committee as a Political System: The Problem of Integration." *American Political Science Review* 56 (June 1962): 310-24.

Fenton, John H. *People and Parties in Politics.* Glenview, Ill.: Scott, Foresman, 1966.

Fiorina, Morris P. *Congress: Keystone of the Washington Establishment.* New Haven, Conn.: Yale Univ. Press, 1977.

Freud, Sigmund, and William C. Bullitt. *Thomas Woodrow Wilson: A Psychological Study.* Boston: Houghton Mifflin, 1967.

Garceau, Oliver, and Corinne Silverman. "A Pressure Group and the Pressured: A Case Report." *American Political Science Review* 48 (Sept. 1954): 672-91.

George, Alexander L. "Assessing Presidential Character." *World Politics* 26 (Jan. 1974): 234-82.

George, Alexander L., and Juliette L. George. *Woodrow Wilson and Colonel House: A Personality Study.* 2d ed. New York: Dover, 1964.

Greenstein, Fred I. "Personality and Politics: Theoretical and Methodological Issues." *Journal of Social Issues* 24 (July 1968).

———. *Personality and Politics.* Chicago: Markham, 1969.

Hermann, Margaret G., ed. *A Psychological Examination of Political Leaders.* New York: Free Press, 1977.

Hoffer, Eric. *The True Believer.* New York: Harper and Row, 1951.

Huitt, Ralph. "The Outsider in the Senate: An Alternative Role." *American Political Science Review* 55 (Sept. 1961): 566-75.

Iremonger, Lucille. *The Fiery Chariot: A Study of British Prime Ministers and the Search for Love.* London: Secker and Warburg, 1970.

Keniston, Kenneth. *Young Radicals.* New York: Harcourt, Brace and World, 1968.

Kirkpatrick, Jeane. *The New Presidential Elite: Men and Women in National Politics.* New York: Russell Sage Foundation and Twentieth Century Fund, 1976.

Knutson, Jeanne N. *The Human Basis of the Polity: A Psychological Study of Political Men.* Chicago: Aldine-Atherton, 1972.

Lasswell, Harold D. *Power and Personality.* New York: Norton, 1948.

―――. *Psychopathology and Politics.* Chicago: Univ. of Chicago Press, 1930.

Leites, Nathan. *On the Game of Politics in France.* Palo Alto, Calif.: Stanford, Univ. Press, 1959.

Maccoby, Michael. *The Gamesman: The New Corporate Leaders.* New York: Simon and Schuster, 1976.

Manley, John F. "The House Committee on Ways and Means: Conflict Management in a Congressional Committee." *American Political Science Review* 59 (Dec. 1965): 927-39.

Maslow, Abraham H. *Motivation and Personality.* New York: Harper, 1954.

Matthews, Donald R. *U.S. Senators and Their World.* New York: Random House, Vintage Books, 1960.

Mayhew, David R. *Congress: The Electoral Connection.* New Haven, Conn.: Yale Univ. Press, 1974.

McClelland, David C. *The Achieving Society.* Princeton, N.J.: Van Nostrand, 1961.

McConaughy, John B. "Certain Personality Factors of State Legislators in South Carolina." *American Political Science Review* 44 (Dec. 1950): 897-903.

Murray, Henry A. *Explorations in Personality.* New York: Oxford Univ. Press, 1938.

Ornstein, Norman J., ed. *Congress in Change.* New York: Praeger, 1975.

Prewitt, Kenneth. "Political Ambitions, Volunteerism, and Electoral Accountability." *American Political Science Review* 64 (Mar. 1970): 5-17.

―――. "Political Socialization and Leadership Selection." *Annals of the American Academy of Political and Social Science* 361 (Sept. 1965): 95-111.

Prewitt, Kenneth, and William Nowlin. "Political Ambitions and the Behavior of Incumbent Politicians." *Western Political Quarterly* 22 (June 1969): 298-308.

Putnam, Robert D. *The Beliefs of Politicians: Ideology, Conflict, and Democracy in Britain and Italy.* New Haven, Conn.: Yale Univ. Press, 1973.

Renshon, Stanley A. *Psychological Needs and Political Behavior: A Theory of Personality and Political Efficacy.* New York: Free Press, 1974.

Riesman, David, Nathan Glazer, and Reuel Denney. *The Lonely Crowd: A Study of the Changing American Character.* Garden City, N.Y.: Doubleday, Anchor Books, 1953.

Rogow, Arnold A., and Harold D. Lasswell. *Power, Corruption and Rectitude.* Englewood Cliffs, N.J.: Prentice-Hall, 1963.

Schlesinger, Joseph A. *Ambition and Politics: Political Careers in the United States.* Chicago: Rand McNally, 1966.

Schoenberger, Robert A. "Conservatism, Personality and Political Extremism." *American Political Science Review* 62 (Sept. 1968): 868-71.

Seligman, Lester. "Political Recruitment and Party Structure." *American Political Science Review* 55 (Mar. 1961): 77-86.

Smith, M. Brewster. "A Map for the Analysis of Personality and Politics." *Journal of Social Issues* 24 (July 1968): 15-28.

Smith, M. Brewster, Jerome Bruner, and Robert White. *Opinions and Personality.* New York: Wiley, 1956.

Snowiss, Leo M. "Congressional Recruitment and Representation." *American Political Science Review* 60 (Sept. 1966); 627-39.

Sorauf, Frank J. *Political Parties in the American System.* Boston: Little, Brown, 1964.

Soule, John W. "Future Political Ambitions and the Behavior of Incumbent State Legislators." *Midwest Journal of Political Science* 13 (Aug. 1969): 439-54.

Soule, John W., and James W. Clarke. "Amateurs and Professionals: A Study of Delegates to the 1968 Democratic National Convention." *American Political Science Review* 64 (Sept. 1970): 888-98.

Tucker, Robert C. "The Georges' Wilson Reexamined: An Essay on Psychobiography." *American Political Science Review* 71 (June 1977): 606-18.

Wahlke, John C., Heinz Eulau, William Buchanan, and LeRoy C. Ferguson. *The Legislative System.* New York: Wiley, 1962.

Wildavsky, Aaron. "The Goldwater Phenomenon: Purists, Politicians, and the Two-Party System." *Review of Politics* 27 (July 1965): 386-413.

Wilson, James Q. *The Amateur Democrat.* Chicago: Univ. of Chicago Press, 1962.

Wolfenstein, E. Victor. *The Revolutionary Personality: Lenin, Trotsky, Gandhi.* Princeton, N.J.: Princeton Univ. Press, 1967.

Index

Adulation incentive: characteristics of, 165–67; personal reinforcement, need for, 166; praise, need for, 165; sensitivity to criticism, 168
Affection-consciousness: in Brazil and Dominican Republic, 167; as source of drive for adulation incentive, 167–68
Age. *See* Entry age
Alienation, 126
Altruism, 50
Ambition, 22
Analytical tendency, 71, 132, 142, 155–57
Anxiety. *See* Guilt anxieties
Autobiography, in incentive analysis, 30, 93

Barber, James David, 12
Bryan, Mary Baird, 43
Bryan, William Jennings, 30–47, 51, 67, 100, 171, 182, 197

Career advancement, 38, 171
Career patterns, of incentive types, 173
Clark, David, 21–29
Colombia, Congress of, 175–76
"Common sense," 109
Competitive drive, 129–34, 154. *See also* Game incentive
Conflict avoidance, incentives and, 79, 84, 97, 167. *See also* Conviviality incentive

Congress: of Colombia, 175–76; of France, 171; of U.S., 174–76. *See also* Legislative behavior
Conscience, attitudes toward, 114, 123. *See also* Expediency
Conscience, 103, 116. *See also* Obligation incentive
Conviviality incentive: "Backslapper" stereotype, 80; characteristics of, 187; compared with adulation type, 167; conflict avoidance, 79, 84, 97, 167; contrast to obligation type, 110–11; courageous self-image, 88–89; desire to be helpful, 87; friendship, emphasis on, 93, 101; helping, enjoyment from, 94; kindness to others, 95; moral convictions, 92–93; need for approval, 79; need for social acceptance, 79; perception of harmony, 80; spectator orientation, 99–101
Corruption, attitudes toward, 114, 123. *See also* Expediency
Coverup, to hide incentives, 23, 34, 77
Cultural influences, 14. *See also* Affection-consciousness

Democratic Conventions, Bryan's participation in: National, of 1892, 35; National, of 1904, 36; National, of 1912, 37

209

Disruptive behavior: in Colombian Congress, 176; in French National Assembly, 171
Disruptiveness: of adulation type, 167; of obligation type, 124, 165; of status type, 173-76
Doctrine, political, importance to mission type of, 163-65
Dogmatism, 52, 164; of obligation type, 107-9
Dupuis, Armand, 105-12
"Duty" orientation, of obligation type, 104

Egocentricity, 37, 131, 144, 166
Election campaigns, attitudes toward: of adulation type, 166; incentive influence on, 175-77; of program type, 64; of status type, 27-28
Enthusiasm for politics, 132, 145
Entry age (into politics): of program types, 76; of status types, 76, 173
Expediency, 25, 45-47
Extremist groups, and mission types, 165

Finley, Peter, 81-92
France, National Assembly of, 171
Franklin, Benjamin, 65-78, 182; *Autobiography of,* 65
French Deputies, 171. See also Congress

Game incentive: characteristics of, 184; comparison to other types, 129-32; competition, need for, 129-34; objectivity, importance of, 133-34; policy, attitude toward, 158, 160; respect for opponents, 136, 154; rules, recognition of and stress on, 142, 155, 157-58, 159-60; strategy and tactics, emphasis on, 131-32, 136-38; winning, need for, 131, 153-54
Glory, 35
Group behavior, incentive influence on, 170, 173-76. See also Legislative behavior; Political behavior, incentive influence on
Guilt anxieties, 102

Hackenburg, Frederick L., 102, 112-27; *A Solitary Parade,* 126
Hammersmith, William, 53-65
Harmonious relations, interest in: of conviviality type, 80, 97; of program type, 73-74
Hart, Gordon, 134-46
Hays, Brooks, 92-101; *A Hotbed of Tranquility,* 92
Hobby, politics as, 64, 75
Hologram analogy, 29
Honesty, 25
House of Representatives, U.S., 175-76. See also Congress

Iconoclasm, 69
Iconoclastic orientation, of program types, 53, 61, 69
Idealism, 13-15
Idealist, 32, 47, 78; behavioral definition of, 32; motivational definition of, 32
"Ideologists," 43-45, 47-48, 49
Idiosyncrasies, 13, 20, 170
Image-building, 65-66; and obligation type, 111; and status type, 66
Incentive analysis, 169-83; and behavior of politicians, 170-73, 179-83; and institutional characteristics, 173-76; and political stability, 176-79. See

also Incentive interpretation, based on interviews; Methodology; Political behavior
Incentive characteristics: adulation type, 165-68; conviviality type, 187-88; game type, 189-90; mission type, 163-65; obligation type, 188-89; program type, 186-87; status type, 185-86
Incentive composition, of institutions and groups, 173-76
Incentive interpretation, based on interviews, 192-94. *See also* Interviews, for incentives; Methodology
Incentives: absence of, 9; axiom, 11; emotional need, 7, 148; of politicians differ, 7; singular for each politician, 8. *See also* Incentive characteristics
Interview questions, for incentives, 194-96
Interviews, for incentives, 5, 9, 28, 77, 89-91, 191-96. *See also* Methodology
Institutional impact of incentives, 173-76
Issues. *See* Policy issues

Legislative behavior: Colombian Congress, 175-76; French National Assembly, 171-72; influence of incentives on speechmaking, committee attendance, disruptive behavior, 170-73; U.S. House of Representatives, 170-77
Legislative structure, influence of incentives on, 173-77
Lipsen, Charles B., 146-61; *Vested Interest,* 146, 149
Lobbyist(s): Hackenburg's attitude toward, 122; Lipsen's attitude as, 149

Loyalty, personal, 41-42

Maccoby, Michael, 18
Mass appeal: and electoral advantage, 175-76; of program type, 64-66; of status type, 66. *See also* Image-building; Publicity-seeking
Methodology, 9; case studies, 14-15; exploratory approach, 6, 9-12, 18; incentive interview techniques, 191-96; incentive relevant autobiography, criteria for, 30, 93; inferring incentives, 20, 28, 77, 89-91; interview questions, 194-96; negation of alternative classifications, 89-91; use of interviews, 5, 9, 20. *See also* Incentive analysis; Political behavior
Mission incentive: centrality of doctrine, 163; characteristics of, 163-65; commitment to transcendental cause, 163; exhilaration from repression, 165; hostility to ideologically similar groups, 164-65; veneration of leader-ideologist, 164
Moral imperatives, 104-8
Moral issues, 46-47
Moral relativism, 158
Motivations, interpretations of: a priori approach, 15-17; biographical approach, 14-15; emotional needs as incentives, 7, 11, 148; evaluational approach, 13; goal explanation of, 179-83; philosophical approach, 16; role of policy goals, 6, 13. *See also* Incentives
Motives, attribution to others by politicians, 24, 55, 120, 125, 136-38. *See also* Political opponents, attitudes toward

Negative attitude toward politics, 145. *See also* Politics, privations of

Objectivity, 132–33, 142, 150
Obligation incentive: aloneness, 106, 125–26; a priori positions, 124; characteristics of, 188–89; denigration, 122; "duty" orientation, 104; guilt anxieties, 102, 123; intolerance, 124; moral imperatives, 104–8; policy analysis, 110, 118; sense of martyrdom, 106, 125; sticking to beliefs, 106
Office-seeking, 22–24, 115, 145
Opponents. *See* Political opponents, attitudes toward
Opportunists, 13–15, 47

Personal approval: adulation type, 166; conviviality type, 79, 166
"Playing the game," 131. *See also* Sports, analogies to
Policy issues: game compared with program, 138–39; game type, 160; incentive related, 49–51; obligation type, 110; program type, 54–57, 67–72; significance to Bryan, 42–43; status type, 25–27, 42–43
Policy making, 60, 72–74, 177–79; comparison of incentive types, 124–25, 178–79; goal explanation of, 180–81. *See also* Policy issues
Political behavior, incentive influence on: contrast with goal explanations, 179–83; examples of influences, 171–73; limitations of incentive explanations, 20, 170, 179. *See also* Legislative behavior; Methodology
Political institutions, influence of incentives on, 173–76

Political opponents, attitudes toward: attribution of motives, 24, 55, 120, 125, 136–38; avoidance of personal attacks, 143; game type, 136–38; keeping your word to, 143; obligation type, 120, 125; program type, 55; respect for, 136–37; status type, 24
Political parties, value of, 142, 144
Political processes, influence of incentives on, 170–73. *See also* Legislative behavior; Political behavior
Political stability, influence of incentives on, 176–79. *See also* Disruptiveness
"Politicians," attitude toward label of: game type, 145; obligation type, 106; traditional views of, 11–12; uniqueness of motivation, 8. *See also* Political opponents, attitudes toward
Politics, privations of: competition, 5; criticism and hostility, 1; danger, 3; financial burdens, 4; public accusations, 1; time pressures, 3
Position-getting: interest of obligation types, 63, 115; interest of status types, 22–24; lack of interest of program types, 63, 77. *See also* Office-seeking
Position taking: on policies, 50; status type, 44–46. *See also* Policy issues
Positive attitude toward politics, 145
Pragmatism, 155–57. *See also* Expediency
Prestige, 24
Prizes, 40–41
Program incentive: characteristics of, 186–87; contrast to

obligation, 110; empiricism, 52; iconoclastic, 53, 61, 69; indifference to criticism, 65; interest in harmonious personal relations, 73–74; interest in policy, 49–50; interest in policy-making process, 72–74; interest in substantive issues, 51–53; lack of interest in position-getting, 63, 77; lack of mass appeal, 64–66; objectivity in, 52; politics as hobby, 75; poor image-building, 65–66

Psychological need, 7; conviviality type, 79; program type, 49. *See also* Incentive characteristics; Incentives

Public image: Bryan as idealist, 32, 43–45; Hays as obligation type, 92; policy-oriented politicians, 49–50

Publicity, 44, 66

Publicity-seeking, 44, 65–66, 153, 171–73

Rectitude, 107, 116

Reformism, Hackenburg experience, 112–26

Role influences, 15

Role playing, 142

Rules: importance of fair play, 159–60; recognition of informal, 142, 155, 157–58. *See also* Game incentive

Self-centeredness, 166–67

Self-confidence, 166; conviviality type, 131; game type, 131, 139

Self-contradiction, 33, 86, 122–23

Self-criticism, 141, 155

Self-deprecation, 87, 96, 98–100, 101. *See also* Conviviality incentive

Self-effacement, 32–34

Self-glorification, 33

Self-image, 164, 167

Self-projection, 24

Self-restraint, 144

Self-sacrifice, 50

Sensitivity to criticism, 33, 39

Sincerity, 24–25, 46

Social acceptance, 82–83

Solipsism, 37

Speech-making, influence of status incentive on, 171

Sports, analogies to, 115, 141; "Big Leagues," 145, 147; coaching, 142; "playing the game," 129–31; sportsmanship, 143; teamwork, 106, 144

Stability. *See* Disruptiveness; Political stability, influence of incentives on

Status incentive: assessments of others' motives, 24; characteristics of, 185–86; compared with adulation, 165; contrast to obligation, 112; egocentric policy involvement, 59–60; emphasis on career, 21–23, 165–67; evaluations of the status of others, 23–24; impact on policy, 177–79; importance of "status" symbols, 166; influence on legislative behavior, 171–76; influence on political stability, 177–79; need for fame, 19; need for recognition, 72–74; personal advancement, 22–24; publicity-seeking, 44, 66; public recognition, 20

Strategies, use of, 28, 38, 72–73 124, 131–32, 141–42, 151–52, 160

Subjectivity, 122

Success, 28

Symbolic politics. *See* Image-building; Publicity-seeking

Tactics. *See* Strategies
Teamwork, 143–44. *See also* Sports, analogies to
Transcendental causes, 163–65
Trustworthiness, 142–43, 159–61

Utopian ideology, 163–65

Wildavsky, Aaron, 17
Winning, importance of, 131, 153–54
Word choice, as an indication of incentive type, 107–8, 141

Augsburg College
George Sverdrup Library
Minneapolis, Minnesota 55454